Building the 2021 Affordable Military

AUTHORS

Clark Murdock
Ryan Crotty
Angela Weaver

A Report of the CSIS International S

June 2014

CSIS | CENTER FOR STRATEGIC &
INTERNATIONAL STUDIES

ROWMAN & LITTLEFIELD
Lanham • Boulder • New York • Toronto • Plymouth, UK

About CSIS

For over 50 years, the Center for Strategic and International Studies (CSIS) has worked to develop solutions to the world's greatest policy challenges. Today, CSIS scholars are providing strategic insights and bipartisan policy solutions to help decisionmakers chart a course toward a better world.

CSIS is a nonprofit organization headquartered in Washington, D.C. The Center's 220 full-time staff and large network of affiliated scholars conduct research and analysis and develop policy initiatives that look into the future and anticipate change.

Founded at the height of the Cold War by David M. Abshire and Admiral Arleigh Burke, CSIS was dedicated to finding ways to sustain American prominence and prosperity as a force for good in the world. Since 1962, CSIS has become one of the world's preeminent international institutions focused on defense and security; regional stability; and transnational challenges ranging from energy and climate to global health and economic integration.

Former U.S. senator Sam Nunn has chaired the CSIS Board of Trustees since 1999. Former deputy secretary of defense John J. Hamre became the Center's president and chief executive officer in April 2000.

CSIS does not take specific policy positions; accordingly, all views expressed herein should be understood to be solely those of the author(s).

ISBN: 978-1-4422-2861-0 (pb); 978-1-4422-2862-7 (eBook)

Center for Strategic & International Studies
1616 Rhode Island Avenue, NW
Washington, DC 20036
202-887-0200 | www.csis.org

Rowman & Littlefield
4501 Forbes Boulevard
Lanham, MD 20706
301-459-3366 | www.rowman.com

Contents

Executive Summary

The post-9/11 U.S. defense drawdown will be significantly deeper than is generally recognized. Because of the dual effect, or "double whammy," of the topline drawdown and the decreasing purchasing power of defense dollars, the military that the Department of Defense (DoD) can afford in 2021 will be smaller across the board, with sharp reductions in capacity in many areas. The question is whether it will be effective as well. To cope with a drawdown of this magnitude, DoD needs to adopt a dramatically different approach to force planning—one that is grounded in the acceptance of budgetary caps established by the Budget Control Act of 2011 (BCA). By adopting the "cost-capped" methodological approach described in this report, DoD can minimize the impact of deep budgetary cuts and provide the military capabilities needed for the strategic realities of 2021 and beyond (2020+).

To cope with a drawdown of this magnitude, the CSIS study team[1] developed over the course of two years a methodological approach for how DoD could minimize the impact of a deep budgetary reduction and provide the military capabilities needed for the strategic realities of 2020+. The CSIS study team also built cost calculators for making trade-off decisions in 2021 with respect to force structure and weapons systems. In this report, the study team uses "cost-capped" methodology and the 2021 cost calculators to generate a set of 2021 alternative militaries, each of which reflects a different strategy, and recommends one. That said, possibly the most important aspect of this report is that it demonstrates the cost-capped methodology in action.

The proposed cost-capped methodology consists of five steps.

Step 1: Set the Starting Point. For the purposes of the exercise, the study team chose the **2012 Pre-Drawdown Force** as a logical starting point. The post-9/11 end strength of the U.S. military peaked in 2010 and started to come down slowly as the United States gradually withdrew from Iraq, despite the subsequent "surge" in Afghanistan. The cost of each 2012 force structure unit is measured in 2013 dollars.

Step 2: Set the End Point. The study team chose 2021 as the end point based on the BCA. The BCA mandates that the second tranche of budget cuts, which are often called the

---

1. Clark Murdock, senior adviser, and Ryan Crotty, fellow, started this study effort in January 2012 and have participated continuously. Kelley Sayler, research associate, participated until she left CSIS in early 2013, and Angela Weaver, research assistant, took her place in early 2013. Ms. Weaver also supported the project during her time as a research intern, as did Raj Pattani. See About the Authors for more information on Clark Murdock, Ryan Crotty, and Angela Weaver.

"sequester cuts" but are actually lower BCA caps (for another $492 billion over nine years, fiscal years 2013–2021), be applied in across-the-board reductions to all DoD programs except for uniformed military personnel. Utilizing the 2021 Force Cost Calculator, which provides (again in 2013 dollars) the cost of each 2021 force structure unit, the default end point is the **2021 Sequester Force**. Cutting everything equally would create the wrong military for the United States in 2021, but such an approach will be attractive both politically and bureaucratically because it sustains today's priorities, which serve many interests both inside and outside DoD.

Step 3: Adjust the 2021 Sequester Force to 2020+ Strategic Realities. Using the 2021 Force Cost Calculator and reengineering the 2021 Sequester Force, the CSIS study team built the **2021 Baseline Force** by adapting the priorities of the 2012 Pre-Drawdown Force to 2020+ strategic realities. Simply projecting a smaller version of the 2012 Pre-Drawdown Force does not create the right military for the strategic realities of 2020 and beyond (2020+):

- The 2021 military should be equipped to respond to the threats of 2021+, not the threats of today. Today's challenges, from other great powers to violent Islamic extremists, have changed greatly in the last decade and will continue to evolve.

- The nature of warfare is constantly evolving, in part because the U.S. military continues to force the pace of innovation. For example, DoD recently announced that its Cyber Mission Force will more than triple in size (from 1,800 to 6,000 people) by the end of 2016.[2]

- As indicated in its 2012 Defense Strategic Guidance and 2014 Quadrennial Defense Review (QDR) report, DoD has committed to sustaining the readiness of its military, maintaining its high-tech edge, and preserving key military competencies such as world-class intelligence, surveillance, and reconnaissance (ISR).

Using the 2021 Sequester Force as the "new normal" would simply reward bureaucratic inertia and political resistance and ignore the U.S. military's proven record of strategic adaptation.

Step 4: Define a Set of Strategic Options (SOs). SO 1 is the 2021 Baseline Force that was built in Step 3, representing today's strategy adapted to 2020+ strategic realities. The cost-capped approach first determines what is affordable and then introduces strategic choice into the equation by defining a set of options that vary from the Baseline Force.

Step 5: Choose One Strategic Option as the 2021 Affordable Military. Analyzing the respective strengths and weaknesses of the strategic options establishes the basis for choosing the **2021 Affordable Military**, which is, indeed, affordable, has adapted to 2021+ strategic realities, and reflects the strategic preferences of a future administration.

---

2. Jon Harper, "Wanted: Cyberwarriors, No Experience or Knowledge Necessary," *Stars and Stripes*, March 29, 2014.

This report applies the cost-capped methodology as a proof of principle. Extensive appendices trace the two-year evolution of the Affordable Military methodology, the development of the 2021 Cost Calculators (both for force structure and modernization), and the rationale for the CSIS study team's list of must-have capabilities for 2020 and beyond.

In addition to the 2021 Baseline Force, force structures and modernization profiles are generated for three additional strategic options: Asia-Pacific Rebalance, Great Power Conflict, and Global Political-Economic-Military Competition. The CSIS study team recommended Great Power Conflict as the most appropriate strategy for the security and fiscal realities of 2020+. However, the intended effect of this study effort is to demonstrate the value of the cost-capped methodology to a Defense Department struggling to cope with the stringent resource constraints imposed by the BCA.

The resource constraints of the "double whammy" are a cause for deep concern. Although defense spending as a whole (base budget and overseas contingencies operations, or OCO) peaked in fiscal year (FY) 2010 (at $730 billion in 2013 dollars) when deployments in Afghanistan were at their highest, DoD's base budget peaked in FY 2012 and with OCO totaled $660 billion in 2013 dollars. In FY 2021 under the budgetary caps imposed by the BCA, the base budget will be $520 billion (again in 2013 dollars), which represents a decline of 21 percent. During this same time period, the defense dollar will have lost 15 percent of its purchasing power because of the aggregate impact of internal cost growth.

The "cost-capped" approach accepts this harsh fiscal reality as a given and attempts to maximize the military utility of a force that is affordable with significantly fewer resources. The cost-capped approach is not very satisfying for strategists, who prefer to define a strategy that fits the strategic context and then ask "how much is enough?" In contrast, the cost-capped approach asks first "how much is affordable" and then develops alternative "strategies" for spending capped resources. Whether that is "enough" or sufficient for the strategic realities of 2020 and beyond is neither known nor assumed.

Introduction

Although defense spending as a whole (both for the base budget and OCO) peaked in FY 2010 (at $730 billion in 2013 dollars) when deployments in Afghanistan were at their highest, DoD's base budget peaked in FY 2012 with an OCO total of $660 billion in 2013 dollars. In FY 2021, under the budgetary caps imposed by the BCA, the budget will be $520 billion (again in 2013 dollars), which represents a decline of 21 percent. During this same time period, the defense dollar will have lost 15 percent of its purchasing power because of the aggregate impact of internal cost growth.[1]

Defense spending started to fall in FY 2011 (Figure 1), reflecting troop withdrawals from Iraq, but the base budget of DoD continued to increase through FY 2012. On 27 January 2009, Secretary of Defense Robert Gates told the Senate Armed Services Committee that "the spigot of defense spending that opened on 9/11 is closing" and that the Department would have to make "hard choices" as it adapted to new fiscal realities.[2] Although Secretary Gates sought defense efficiencies from the beginning of the Obama administration—by the time he left DoD in July 2011, he claimed to have identified $230 billion[3] in projected savings— the initial impact was to reduce the rate of growth only in DoD's base budget. In July 2011, Congress passed the BCA, which mandated a first tranche of defense budget cuts (imposed by the "BCA caps") totaling $487 billion over 10 years (FY 2012–FY 2021). This launched DoD on its fourth defense drawdown since the United States demobilized after World War II.

This defense drawdown will be much deeper than is generally recognized. There is no question that the military that DoD can afford in 2021, which we call the **2021 Affordable Military**, will be significantly smaller with deep reductions in many areas. The question is

---

1. As discussed in Appendix D, the impact of the 21 percent topline decline and 15 percent in internal cost growth is not applied equally across each segment of the budget because of the variable impact of OCO on each account and thus cannot be aggregated directly to a 35 percent total impact on capability and capacity. The high percentage of war funding that applies to force structure costs in 2012 in particular mitigates the impact of the topline decline on the cuts to force structure as OCO comes down. In the interests of not inflating the costs of these units with the additional wartime costs of combat pay, pay for reserve units on active duty, and operating and maintaining units overseas in a combat environment, the costs calculated for force structure units use base budget costs only. Thus, the impact on the force structure for the sequester force is driven nearly entirely by internal cost growth. It is likely that this actually *understates* the 2021 force costs, as most commentators have noted that there are many costs in the OCO budget that will have to be reabsorbed in the base budget as war funding draws down. Without the ability to quantify exactly what those costs are, the CSIS study team has not incorporated them.

2. Jen Dimascio, "Gates: Afghanistan Should Be Priority," *Politico,* January 27, 2009, http://www.politico .com/news/stories/0109/18036.html.

3. See Appendix C.

whether it will be effective as well. To cope with a drawdown of this magnitude, the CSIS study team developed over the course of two years a methodological approach for how DoD could minimize the impact of a deep budgetary reduction and provide the military capabilities needed for the strategic realities of 2020 and beyond (2020+).[4] The CSIS study team also built cost calculators for making trade-off decisions in 2021 with respect to force structure and weapons systems. In this report, the team uses the "cost-capped" methodology and the 2021 cost calculators to generate a set of 2021 alternative militaries, each of which reflects a different strategy, and recommends one as the 2021 Affordable Force. In short, the two-year Affordable Military project, which began in January 2012, has generated three deliverables—a methodology for coping with a deep defense drawdown, analytic tools for estimating costs in 2021, and a recommendation for the strategic option that constitutes the "least bad" 2021 Affordable Military.

The traditional "strategy-driven" approach taken by defense strategists and planners asks "how much is enough" to resource the preferred strategy. In contrast, the "cost-capped" approach accepts as given the legislatively mandated budgetary ceilings and the seemingly inexorable internal cost growth of the past decades and asks, "How much is affordable?" Whether this is, indeed, sufficient for U.S. security needs in 2020+ is not known (or assumed) today. The "administration after next" will learn, often the hard way, how to find a sustainable balance between DoD's military means and U.S. strategic ends. And, much like any prudent household in the midst of a Great Recession, the first step is accepting the fiscal ground truth of how much military capability and capacity is affordable with fewer and weaker defense dollars.

The intellectual foundations of the five-step cost-capped approach, which is briefly described in the Executive Summary, are in the appendices, where the study team presents the evolution of methodology for building the 2021 Affordable Military, the 2021 cost calculators for force structure and modernization, and the team's assessment of the strategic realities for 2020 and beyond (2020+). After stating briefly the argument for why the Defense Department needs to adopt the cost-capped approach for coping with a deep defense drawdown, this report will implement its recommended approach as a proof-of-principle demonstration.

The Defense Budget's Economic Vise: Drawing Down while Hollowing Out from Within

Although the legislatively mandated defense budget cuts expire in FY 2021, the downward pressure on the defense budget topline is likely to be unrelenting. As illustrated in Figure 1, the tradespace for discretionary spending is being squeezed out by mandatory spending—which includes spending on veteran benefits, income security, social security, Medicare, and Medicaid—and interest payments. If current trends continue, including the overall growth rate of total federal spending planned for FY 2013–FY 2017, there will be no

---

4. The CSIS cost-capped methodology is chronicled in detail in Appendix C.

Figure 1. Long-term Pressure on the Defense Topline

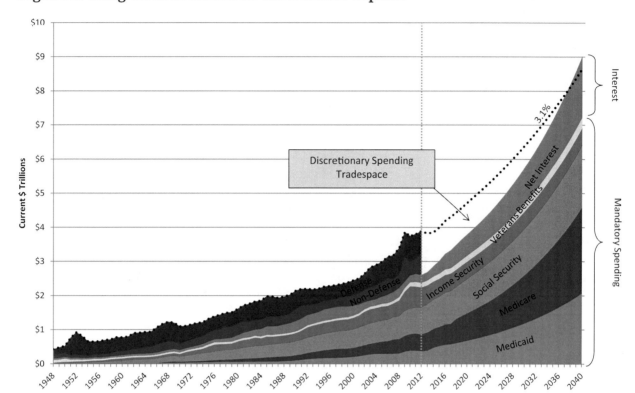

room for discretionary spending, either defense or nondefense, by 2036. In a real sense, the debate over whether the BCA sequester-level cuts will be lifted by FY 2021 is moot, because the larger vise on the U.S. federal budget—caused by the growing gap between entitlement programs spending and government revenue—will result in a deep defense drawdown.

As portrayed in Figure 2, the legislatively mandated BCA cuts would result in a defense drawdown of about 31 percent from the FY 2010 peak to the FY 2017 trough, resulting in a drawdown that at first glance appears less severe, since it is actually below the historical range (from 43 percent after the Korean War to 33 percent after Vietnam). The BCA imposed two tranches of topline cuts: $487 billion from FY 2012 to FY 2021 and, if Congress failed (which it did) to reach an agreement on a deficit reduction package, $430 billion from FY 2013 to FY 2021.[5] Although defense spending as a whole (the base budget and OCO) peaked in FY 2010 at the height of the U.S. troop deployment to Afghanistan, the base budget continued to grow until FY 2012, when the first tranche of BCA budget caps kicked in. The topline decline in DoD's defense budget from FY 2012 (the post-9/11 peak in the base budget) will total 21 percent by FY 2021.

Figure 2 also suggests why this defense drawdown is different from the others. In the past, drawdowns ended below $400 billion in constant 2013 dollars; this one will bottom

---

5. In January 2013, the BCA "sequester cuts" were modified slightly, resulting in a nine-year total reduction of $492 billion in 2013 dollars. The January 2014 Bipartisan Budget Agreement raised the limits by $22.5 billion in FY 2014 and $9 billion in FY 2015, but the full sequester cuts (to the original BCA caps) of $52 billion per year resume in FY 2016.

Figure 2. Defense Drawdowns Compared

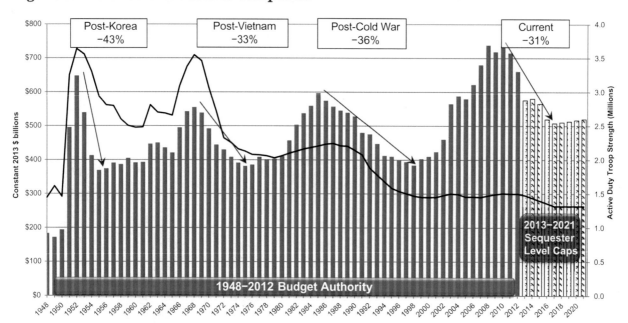

out at over $500 billion. In FY 2017, even though DoD is spending over $100 billion more, it will "buy" an active duty force that is 34 percent smaller than in 1978 and six percent smaller than in 2000. This means not just fewer defense dollars but also a "weaker" defense dollar in terms of its purchasing power.

The aggregate impact of growth (above inflation) in the cost of personnel, health care, operations and maintenance (O&M), and acquisition results in a defense dollar that "buys" less and less capability. As DoD pointed out in its January 2012 white paper on the defense budget, personnel costs in the base budget "increased by nearly 90 percent or about 30 percent above inflation [since 2001], while the number of military personnel has increased by only about 3 percent."[6] O&M costs per active duty service member are also increasing steadily:

- Between 1980 and 2001, they increased from $55,000 to $105,000 (in constant 2012 dollars);

- In DoD's FY 2012 base budget request, they are estimated at $147,000 per active duty service member and are projected to "grow at more than one and one-half times the historical (pre-2001) rate through the (FYDP) period, reaching $161,000 in 2016."[7]

The aggregate impact of internal cost growth will "hollow out" the defense budget from within by 15 percent over FY 2012–FY 2021.

This 10-year loss of capacity—that is, the difference of how much capability the 2021 defense budget can purchase in comparison to 2012—may not be all there is to the post-9/11

---

6. U.S. Department of Defense, *Overview—United States Department of Defense Fiscal Year 2013 Budget Request*, 43.

7. Congressional Budget Office, "Long Term Implications of the 2012 Future Years Defense Program," June 2011.

drawdown, because the pressure for further reductions may continue (see Figure 2 for historical comparisons) and the Defense Department has not yet demonstrated that it can control internal cost growth. No question, these are hard fiscal realities. "Wishing and hoping" they will go away is not a strategy, as it leaves a DoD in denial unprepared in the event that they don't go away. In contrast, the cost-capped approach takes the economic vise on the defense budget as given. This enables DoD to better prepare for a deep defense drawdown; it also helps make a more compelling case for the deleterious impact on national security caused by the continued political dysfunction over government taxation and spending.

Implementing the Cost-Capped Approach for a Deep Defense Drawdown

What follows is the study team's application of the cost-capped methodology and the 2021 cost calculators to develop alternative militaries, each reflecting a different strategic option, as the basis for choosing the 2021 Affordable Military.

Step 1: Set the Starting Point. The study team's first endeavor was to understand the 2012 Pre-Drawdown Force[8] and to describe it succinctly in terms of force structure units and associated costs. Table 1 displays the 2012 force structure in its key units, along with their unit costs (expressed in 2013 constant dollars) in 2012 and 2021. Although there were important differences in strategic emphasis in each of the key strategy documents—the 2010 QDR report, the 2012 Defense Strategic Guidance (DSG), and the 2014 QDR report—the underlying approach taken to force planning was similar, namely, to maintain a robust portfolio of military capabilities as the foundation of U.S. global leadership.[9] As Secretary Robert Gates said in his preface to the 2010 QDR, "the United States needs a broad portfolio of military capabilities with maximum versatility across the widest possible spectrum of conflict."[10]

The "portfolio" approach to sizing and shaping the force stresses the importance of providing a robust set of military options to the president, who makes the strategic choices on when and where to use military force. This capabilities-based approach to force planning was sustained in the 2012 DSG and 2014 QDR, although the strains caused by increasing fiscal pressure were increasingly acknowledged.

Through these statements, DoD is signaling that the portfolio approach to force planning that underlies the 2012 Pre-Drawdown Force will be jeopardized by the imposition of BCA "sequester cuts." Implicitly, DoD is arguing that U.S. global leadership will be undermined if, as the Affordable Military methodology assumes, the BCA-mandated budget

---

8. As discussed in Appendix D, modernization (RDT&E and procurement) is not analyzed on an annual basis (similar to the approach taken on force structure) but is treated as a cumulative FY 2012–FY 2021 stream of funds that support each acquisition program and annual levels of effort for RDT&E. The FY 2021 Baseline Force, as well as the alternative Strategic Options, will have an associated modernization profile for how RDT&E, plus procurement dollars, are spent.

9. Department of Defense, "Sustaining U.S. Global Leadership: Priorities for 21st Century Defense," January 2012.

10. Department of Defense, *2010 Quadrennial Defense Review*, February 2010, i.

Table 1. The 2012 Pre-Drawdown Force

Force Structure Units	No. of 2012 Force Structure Units	2012 Unit Cost (constant $M)	2021 Unit Cost (constant $M)
Active Army			
Heavy BCT	17	$1,084	$1,296
Infantry BCT	20	$1,009	$1,207
Stryker BCT	8	$1,232	$1,473
Army SOF Battalions	23	$235	$280
Combat Aviation Brigades	12	$532	$638
Army Reserve Component			
Heavy BCT	7	$751	$915
Infantry BCT	20	$697	$849
Stryker BCT	1	$844	$1,029
Combat Aviation Brigades	8	$483	$601
Active Navy			
Aircraft Carriers (Excluding Aviation)	11	$1,254	$1,447
Surface Combatants	110	$91	$115
Amphibious Ships	30	$241	$306
Nuclear Attack Submarines (SSN)	54	$79	$100
Ballistic Missile Submarines (SSBN)	14	$134	$170
Missile Submarines (SSGN)	4	$134	$170
Naval Aviation	10	$1,236	$1,568
Naval Special Warfare Teams	15	$112	$137
Active Marine Corps			
Infantry Regiments	11	$1,264	$1,547
Marine Air Groups	11	$477	$585
Special Operations Battalions	3	$180	$219
Active Air Force			
Bombers	96	$69	$83
Fighters	648	$24	$29
Transport/Tankers	438	$30	$36
Aerial ISR	215	$9	$11
Special Operations Battalions	5	$916	$1,117
ICBMs	450	$6	$8
Global Force Enabling Architecture	1	$4,756	$5,825
Air Force Reserve Component			
Fighters	450	$10	$13
Transport/Tanker	516	$17	$21

DoD's Growing Concern about Its Force Planning Assumptions

> As we end today's wars and reshape our Armed Forces, we will ensure that our military is agile, flexible, and ready for the full range of contingencies.
>
> —President Barack Obama

> This country is at a strategic turning point after a decade of war and, therefore, we are shaping a Joint Force for the future that will be smaller and leaner, but will be agile, flexible, ready, and technologically advanced. . . . It will have a global presence emphasizing the Asia-Pacific and the Middle East, while still ensuring our ability to maintain our defense commitments to Europe, and strengthening alliances and partnerships across all regions. It will preserve our ability to conduct the missions we judge most important to protecting core national interests: defeating al-Qa'ida and its affiliates; succeeding in current conflicts; deterring and defeating aggression by adversaries, including those seeking to deny our power projection; countering weapons of mass destruction; effectively operating in cyberspace, space and across all domains; maintaining a safe and effective nuclear deterrent; and protecting the homeland. —Secretary Leon Panetta

> [G]iven that we cannot predict how the strategic environment will evolve with absolute certainty, we will maintain a broad portfolio of military capabilities that, in the aggregate, offer versatility across the range of missions described above. The Department will make clear distinctions both *among* the key sizing and shaping missions listed above and *between* those mission areas of the defense program [emphasis in original].
>
> —2012 Defense Strategic Guidance

reductions are implemented. A key issue that will have to be addressed in assessing any of the 2021 Strategic Options, including the 2021 Baseline Force, is whether they provide sufficient capacity to support U.S. global leadership.

Step 2: Set the End Point. The study team set the end point for 2021 based on the BCA. In Table 2, the BCA-mandated cuts (both tranches) are applied against the cost (in 2013 constant dollars) in FY 2021 of the FY 2012 Pre-Drawdown Force. These sequester-level cuts are applied in the "meat axe," across-the-board fashion mandated by the BCA and (when divided by the 2021 cost per unit) yield the "2021 Sequester Force" with its many partially funded force units.

The Defense Department would never implement a drawdown in this manner—cutting everything (but military personnel) equally, retaining fractions of a force structure unit, and so on—but it is a useful point of comparison because it constitutes today's capability priorities

DoD's Growing Concern about Its Force Planning Assumptions (cont'd)

[Although committed to ensuring "that the U.S. Armed Forces remain the preeminent global force of the future," the] QDR describes the tough choices we are making in a period of fiscal austerity to maintain the world's finest fighting force. These include reducing force structure in order to protect and expand critical capabilities, modernizing the forces, and investing in readiness. Although the future force will be smaller, it will be ready, capable, and able to project power over great distances.

—Secretary Chuck Hagel

[T]he impact of "sequestration-level cuts":

. . . over the near-, mid-, and long-term [sequestration-level cuts] would have an even more negative impact on the Department's ability to shape events globally.

. . . we would be unable to continue participating at current levels of joint training and exercises that are central to our relationships with allies and partners.

. . . [sequestration-level cuts] would also lead to significant risk in the Department's ability to project power and to win decisively in future conflicts. The Department would have less ability to deter conflict and would face challenges in being able to defeat an adversary quickly if called upon to engage in major combat.

Critical modernization programs would also be broken under sequestration-level cuts, creating deficiencies in the technological capability of our forces despite the requirement that they be able to respond to a wide variety of threats, including substantial A2/AD and cyberspace challenges, as well as threats posed by adversaries employing innovative combinations of modern weaponry and asymmetric tactics.

Finally, . . . the Department would be forced to make a number of non-strategic decisions [such as cutting a carrier, a nuclear attack sub, etc.] with negative impacts for U.S. interests. . . . Doing so would undermine a core competitive advantage for the United States, decreasing our ability to engage globally, project power, deter conflict and decisively win against potential adversaries.

—2014 Quadrennial Defense Review Report

Table 2. The 2021 Sequester Force

Force Structure Units	No. of 2012 Force Structure Units	2021 Unit Cost (constant $M)	2021 Sequester Force
Active Army			
Heavy BCT	17	$1,296	14.6
Infantry BCT	20	$1,207	17.2
Stryker BCT	8	$1,473	6.9
Army SOF Battalions	23	$280	19.8
Combat Aviation Brigades	12	$638	10.3
Army Reserve Component			
Heavy BCT	7	$915	6.0
Infantry BCT	20	$849	17.2
Stryker BCT	1	$1,029	0.9
Combat Aviation Brigades	8	$601	6.9
Active Navy			
Aircraft Carriers (Excluding Aviation)	11	$1,447	9.5
Surface Combatants	110	$115	94.7
Amphibious Ships	30	$306	25.8
Nuclear Attack Submarines (SSN)	54	$100	46.5
Ballistic Missile Submarines (SSBN)	14	$170	12.1
Missile Submarines (SSGN)	4	$170	3.4
Naval Aviation	10	$1,568	8.6
Naval Special Warfare Teams	15	$137	12.9
Active Marine Corps			
Infantry Regiments	11	$1,547	9.5
Marine Air Groups	11	$585	9.5
Special Operations Battalions	3	$219	2.6
Active Air Force			
Bombers	96	$83	82.7
Fighters	648	$29	557.9
Transport/Tankers	438	$36	377.1
Aerial ISR	215	$11	185.1
Special Operations Battalions	5	$1,117	4.3
ICBMs	450	$8	387.5
Global Force Enabling Architecture	1	$5,825	0.9
Air Force Reserve Component			
Fighters	450	$13	387.5
Transport/Tanker	516	$21	444.3

Figure 3. Must-Have Capabilities Needed in 2020–2030

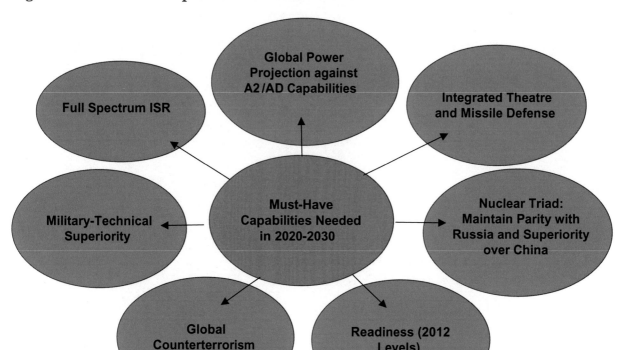

(as expressed in force structure units) that are affordable in FY 2021 dollars. In a sense, the FY 2021 Sequester Force is the default end point created by bureaucratic inertia, political gridlock, and the mechanical implementation of the BCA.[11] Although the 2021 Sequester Force would never actually exist, it provides a reference point for the 2021 Baseline Force.

Step 3: Adjust the 2021 Sequester Force to 2020+ Strategic Realities. The study team created the 2021 Baseline Force by adapting the 2021 Sequester Force (increasing or decreasing specific force structure units) to its analysis of the strategic realities of 2020 and beyond (2020+)—changes in the international security environment and the nature of warfare—and likely actions that DoD will take to maintain key military competencies.[12] With the help of working group and subject matter expert (SME) feedback, the CSIS study team developed a demand-driven list of "must-have capabilities" that any 2021 military will need independent of the strategic proclivities of future administrations. This is displayed in Figure 3.

The Department of Defense is an adaptive organization that responds to changes in the security environment and the evolution of warfare. The metastasizing threat of violent Islamic extremism has provoked a steady, seemingly permanent increase in counterterrorism

---

11. We could have presented a similar table for modernization—with columns for acquisition programs, unit costs in FY 2012–FY 2021, and quantities purchased for both the 2012 Pre-Drawdown Force and 2021 Sequester Force, but it would have been for illustrative purposes only, as DoD would never have implemented a drawdown in this manner.
12. See Appendix E for the detailed analysis.

capabilities (from direct-action special operations forces to unmanned aerial systems of all types). The rapid increase in DoD cyber capabilities, both offensive and defensive, are both responding to and driving the pace of military innovation. The frustration of the American people with the costs, broadly defined, of the U.S. interventions in Iraq and Afghanistan has caused DoD (as announced in the 2012 DSG) to no longer size the force for large-scale, long-duration stability operations, although it will retain the knowledge to regenerate if necessary.

This list of must-have capabilities should be viewed as a "living document" that changes as 2020+ strategic realities evolve. This list of 2020+ must-have capabilities reflected the cumulative effects of changes in the international security environment (e.g., the rise of near-peer competitors and the persistent challenge posed by violent Islamic extremists) and changes in the evolution of warfare (e.g., the growing importance of cyber and space, and the continuing role of nuclear weapons), as well as the sustainment of key U.S. military competencies (e.g., superior ISR and technological superiority).

"Cheat Sheet" for Adapting to 2020+ Strategic Realities

- Increase above 2021 Sequester Force levels
  - ISR capabilities of all the services
    - Superior Situational Awareness is a key U.S. competency
  - S&T, RDT&E
    - Maintain technical superiority
  - SOF direct action
    - Prime CT mission
  - Air Force long-range capabilities
    - Needed to counter anti-access/area-denial (A2/AD) capability
    - Includes transport
  - Army Reserve components
    - Offset deeper Army active cuts; reversibility hedge
  - U.S. Marine Corps force structure and acquisition program to FY 2012 levels
    - Reflects political realities and the dollars involved are not very large

- Maintain at 2021 Sequester Force level
  - Space
  - BMD
  - Unmanned Aerial Systems (UAS)
    - More emphasis to long-range and stealth
  - Nuclear triad

- Everything else is a bill payer

The 2021 Force Cost Calculator first determined the FY 2021 cost of FY 2012 capabilities, applied the across-the-board sequester cut, and then translated that dollar figure into 2012 Sequester Force units and programs. This "cut drill" reduced the FY 2021 cost of the FY 2012 Pre-Drawdown Force to the FY 2021 cost of the Sequester Force. It also used the "meat axe" approach adopted by the Budget Control Act of 2011, that is, reducing all DoD activities by the same percentage. Instead of using this mindless approach (and the 2021 Sequester Force) as the baseline, the CSIS study team adapted the Sequester Force to 2020+ strategic realities. Over repeated iterations, the CSIS study team developed a "cheat sheet" for the many decisions made as elements of the 2021 Sequester Force, both its force structure and modernization profile, were increased or decreased. Like the must-have capabilities, the cheat sheet is a "living document" that represents commonsense, relatively nonstrategic adaptations to changing strategic realities, not variations in strategy. It is an affordable version of the current force that has adapted to changing strategic realities.

In summary, Step 3 defines a 2021 Baseline Force that is "cost capped"—that is, that stays within the sequester-level limits imposed by the BCA and is purchased with weaker FY 2021 defense dollars—and reflects today's priorities (as expressed in the FY 2012 Pre-Drawdown Force) but is adjusted to 2020 and beyond strategic realities.[13] Special operations forces were increased across the board (sometimes above 2012 levels) and Marine force structure was sustained at 2012 levels, which reflects both military judgment (the Marines are a small, crisis-response force) and political reality (the Marine force structure has been mandated by Congress). The loss of carriers was limited to two (from 11 to 9), but the price was a larger cut in surface combatants. Underwater assets (attack and missile-carrying subs) were sustained at 2012 levels, and the nuclear triad was preserved at New START levels. The largest bill payer was active Army force structure, although Air Force force structure (with the exception of bombers and ISR of all types) took a somewhat heavier hit than other force structure elements. The following tables reflect these decisions.

Step 4: Define a Set of Strategic Options. The approach taken toward building a set of strategic options is fairly straightforward: Take the 2021 Baseline Force from Step 3 and develop a set of alternative militaries (in terms of force structure and weapons systems) that are also "cost capped" but represent significantly different strategies for addressing 2020+ strategic realities. Implementing this construct, however, proved far from simple, and the set of strategic options anchored to the 2021 Baseline Force evolved over the course of the study effort.[14] The CSIS study team settled on the following set of four strategic options, outlined in the following tables and depicted visually in Figure 4.

---

13. The 2021 cost calculators for force structure and modernization are discussed in depth in Appendix D.

14. For example, the set of strategic options included a separate one for U.S. technological superiority (see Appendix C), which envisioned increasing the percentage of the defense budget devoted to RDT&E, particularly S&T, so that the United States was driving the pace of military innovation. Maintaining its high-tech edge has always been an American military competency—DoD spends more than eight times as much on military research and development as its nearest competitor and devotes over 10 percent of its defense budget on RDT&E—and will continue to do so in the 2021 Baseline Force and any of its strategic alternatives. However, in the event of a great power competition among the United States, Russia, and China, the United States could choose to ramp up its investment to ensure that it remains technologically superior to its modernizing near-peer competitors.

Table 3. The 2021 Baseline Force: Force Structure

Force Structure Units	2012 Force Structure Units	2021 Sequester Force	2021 Baseline Force
Active Army			
Heavy BCT	17	14.6	8
Infantry BCT	20	17.2	16
Stryker BCT	8	6.9	4
Army SOF Battalions	23	19.8	23
Combat Aviation Brigades	12	10.3	6
Army Reserve Component			
Heavy BCT	7	6.0	9
Infantry BCT	20	17.2	20
Stryker BCT	1	0.9	1
Combat Aviation Brigades	8	6.9	8
Active Navy			
Aircraft Carriers (Excluding Aviation)	11	9.5	9
Surface Combatants	110	94.7	76
Amphibious Ships	30	25.8	26
Nuclear Attack Submarines (SSN)	54	46.5	54
Ballistic Missile Submarines (SSBN)	14	12.1	10
Missile Submarines (SSGN)	4	3.4	4
Naval Aviation	10	8.6	8
Naval Special Warfare Teams	15	12.9	22
Active Marine Corps			
Infantry Regiments	11	9.5	11
Marine Air Groups	11	9.5	11
Special Operations Battalions	3	2.6	3
Active Air Force			
Bombers	96	82.7	90
Fighters	648	557.9	520
Transport/Tankers	438	377.1	355
Aerial ISR	215	185.1	200
Special Operations Battalions	5	4.3	5
ICBMs	450	387.5	400
Global Force Enabling Architecture	1	0.9	1.5
Air Force Reserve Component			
Fighters	450	387.5	400
Transport/Tanker	516	444.3	500

Table 4. The 2021 Baseline Force: Modernization

Program	2012 MDAP Modernization Plan	2021 Sequester Force	2021 Baseline Force
KC-46A	94	84.7	82
LCS	31	27.9	24
P-8A	104	93.7	84
Virginia-class SSN	16	14.4	15
V-22	177	159.5	177
CVN-78	2	1.8	2
DDG-51	12	10.8	10
F-35A	689	621.0	605
F-35B	131	118.1	115
F-35C	120	108.2	105
BMDS	100	90.1	88
UH-60M	667	601.2	536
CH-53K	72	64.9	62
E-2D Advanced Hawkeye	60	54.1	60
LRSB	1	0.9	1
SSBN(X)	1	0.9	1
SBIRS	2	1.8	2
C-130J	47	42.4	41
CH-47F	210	189.3	160
MQ-9 Reaper	245	220.8	221
HC/MC-130 Recap	84	75.7	84
WIN-T Increment-3	1903	1,715.2	1713
AEHF	2	1.8	2
Patriot-MEADS CAP	718	647.2	646
H-1 Upgrades	218	196.5	218
AH-64E Remanufacture	431	388.5	300
LHA 6	1	0.9	1
SM-6	1300	1,171.7	1170
MQ-4C Triton	35	31.5	31
Trident II	24	21.6	21

- Option 1—Baseline Force
  - Today's priorities but in capacities affordable in FY 2021 and adjusted for 2021 strategic realities (that is, addressing 2020+ threats, changes in the nature of warfare, and sustaining key American military competencies).
    - The logic for the changes made to the 2021 Sequester Force in building the 2021 Baseline Force is covered in Step 3. The additional militaries in Options 2–4 were adapted from this baseline.

Figure 4. Building the 2021 Affordable Military

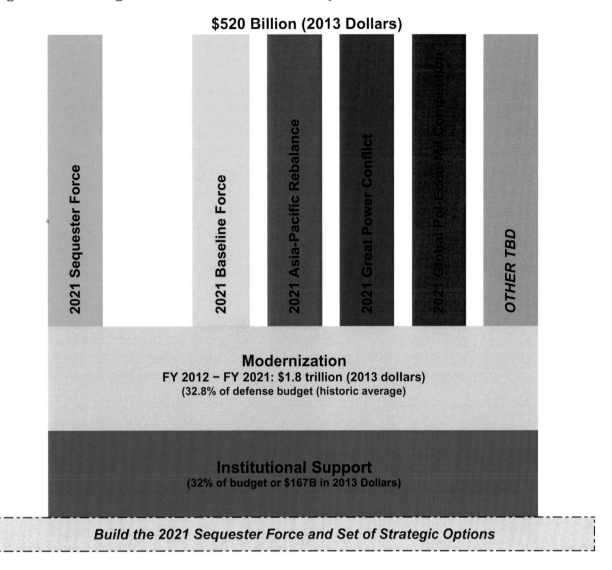

$520 Billion (2013 Dollars)

2021 Sequester Force

2021 Baseline Force

2021 Asia-Pacific Rebalance

2021 Great Power Conflict

2021 Global Pol-Econ-Mil Competition

OTHER TBD

Modernization
FY 2012 − FY 2021: $1.8 trillion (2013 dollars)
(32.8% of defense budget (historic average)

Institutional Support
(32% of budget or $167B in 2013 Dollars)

Build the 2021 Sequester Force and Set of Strategic Options

- Option 2—Asia-Pacific Rebalance
  - Ever since it was incorporated in the 2012 DSG, DoD has been criticized for "not walking the Asian pivot walk." This option reflects a significant reorientation of the U.S. military's force structure (and modernization) toward the Asia-Pacific, both for countering China's growing anti-access/area-denial (A2/AD) capability and to reassure its Asian allies through growing presence—largely U.S. naval and Marine presence.
  - Force Structure/Weapons Implications (in contrast to Baseline Force):
    - More: Naval surface (including a carrier, additional LCS, DDG-51s, and FC-35Cs), Marine regiments and aviation (for Australia-like deployments through the region), acceleration of new bomber.

- Less: Army heavy BCTs, Air Force fighters, slower modernization of nuclear triad (reflects China's relative de-emphasis of nuclear capabilities), missile defense (both theater and national).

- Option 3—Great Power Conflict
  - DoD focuses on enhanced capabilities to deter, defend, and coerce its near-peer competitors and considerably less on presence (in contrast to the Asia-Pacific Rebalance) to assure its allies and friends. "Regional rogues" are treated as lesser-included cases.
    - During the Cold War, when the United States spent two to three times as much of its GDP on defense than it does now, DoD could afford to invest heavily in both preparing for war and presence. Under the sequester-level budget caps, DoD can do this selectively (see Option 2) but not globally. With respect to U.S. global capabilities under the BCA caps, priority must be given either to "warfighting" preparations (Option 3) or presence (Option 4).
    - This SO also diverts $10 billion away from force structure to increase procurement by $3 billion and S&T spending by 50 percent.[15] This aggressive investment in modernization is aimed at sustaining the U.S. high-tech edge versus Russia and China. This amounts to a 16 percent increase from the $63.5 billion (in 2013 dollars) spent on RDT&E in the Baseline Force (and the other options).
  - Force Structure/Weapons Implications (in contrast to Baseline Force):
    - More: Even more accelerated bomber program than in the Asia-Pacific Rebalance (including a second bomber variant), undersea (attack subs), nuclear modernization (to keep pace with Russians and Chinese), national missile defense, aerial and space ISR, Army heavy BCTs (for trip-wire deployments on China/Russian borders), direct-action SOF.
    - Less: Naval surface (two fewer carriers, LCS, DDG-51), naval aviation (F-35Cs, P-8A), Air Force fighters (shorter-range assets vulnerable to near-peer A2/AD).

- Option 4—Global Political-Economic-Military Competition
  - The U.S. government relies on a holistic approach, including an increased reliance on development made possible by diverting $25 billion (in constant 2013 dollars) from Modernization to State/AID for increased foreign assistance. The four-year ramp-up in development aid to a FY 2021 total of $10 billion would represent roughly a 25 percent increase over current level of funding and could provide additional funds to the Millennium Challenge Corporation, the Climate Change Adaptation Fund, Internet freedom activities, and many other foreign assistance programs.
    - This "soft power" option takes a "whole of government" approach to its internationalist stance, including relying more on U.S. global presence provided by Army light infantry and special operations forces to engage in indirect activities (building partnership capacity, training, etc.)

---

15. In the 2021 Baseline Force, S&T is approximately $14 billion in 2013 dollars, which approximates the historical average of spending on S&T at 2.5 percent of the total defense budget.

Table 5. Strategic Options: Force Structure

Force Structure Units	2012 Force Structure Units	2021 Baseline Force	Asia-Pacific	Great Power Conflict	Global Political-Economic-Military Competition
Active Army					
Heavy BCT	17	8	4	10	4
Infantry BCT	20	16	16	13	19
Stryker BCT	8	4	4	3	4
Army SOF Battalions	23	23	20	23	30
Combat Aviation Brigades	12	6	4	5	6
Army Reserve Component					
Heavy BCT	7	9	10	11	10
Infantry BCT	20	20	20	21	20
Stryker BCT	1	1	1	2	1
Combat Aviation Brigades	8	8	6	7	6
Active Navy					
Aircraft Carriers (Excluding Aviation)	11	9	10	7	9
Surface Combatants	110	76	80	60	100
Amphibious Ships	30	26	30	14	26
Nuclear Attack Submarines (SSN)	54	54	54	60	40
Ballistic Missile Submarines (SSBN)	14	10	10	14	8
Missile Submarines (SSGN)	4	4	5	4	3
Naval Aviation	10	8	9	6	8
Naval Special Warfare Teams	15	22	22	22	22
Active Marine Corps					
Infantry Regiments	11	11	13	11	11
Marine Air Groups	11	11	13	11	11
Special Operations Battalions	3	3	3	3	4
Active Air Force					
Bombers	96	90	90	96	70
Fighters	648	520	500	400	406
Transport/Tankers	438	355	355	380	355
Aerial ISR	215	200	214	240	500
Special Operations Battalions	5	5	4	4	6
ICBMs	450	400	400	400	300
Global Force Enabling Architecture	1	1.5	1.5	2	2
Air Force Reserve Component					
Fighters	450	400	400	400	400
Transport/Tanker	516	500	500	500	500

Note: The Great Power Conflict strategic option force structure sums to $10 billion less on an annual basis than the other options. Because of the emphasis on technology development noted in the description above, $10 billion has been diverted to pay for increased RDT&E. $7 billion of that would be directed at S&T functions, while $3 billion is moved into the modernization pot (below).

Table 6. 2021 Strategic Options: Weapon Systems

Force Structure Connection	Program	2012 MDAP Modernization Plan	2021 Baseline Force	Asia-Pacific Rebalance	Great Power Conflict	Global Political-Economic-Military Competition
Tanker	KC-46A	94	82	82	100	90
Surface Combatant	LCS	31	24	35	20	40
Naval Aviation	P-8A	104	84	94	80	84
SSN	Virginia-class SSN	16	15	15	19	13
Marine Air Group	V-22	177	177	199	177	177
Carrier	CVN-78	2	2	3	0	2
Surface Combatant	DDG-51	12	10	14	8	12
Fighter	F-35A	689	605	400	400	600
Marine Air Group	F-35B	131	115	140	100	115
Naval Aviation	F-35C	120	105	122	80	105
Missile Defense	BMDS	100	88	80	82	70
Combat Aviation Brigade	UH-60M	667	536	400	350	600
Marine Air Group	CH-53K	72	62	80	40	50
Naval Aviation	E-2D Advanced Hawkeye	60	60	60	40	55
Bomber	LRSB	1	1	2	3	1
SSBN	SSBN(X)	1	1	0	1	0
GFEM	SBIRS	2	2	1	3	2
Lift	C-130J	47	41	30	41	50
Combat Aviation Brigade	CH-47F	210	160	121	160	180
Aerial ISR	MQ-9 Reaper	245	221	180	230	221
Special Operations	HC/MC-130 Recap	84	84	70	84	90
Brigade Combat Team	WIN-T Increment-3	1,903	1,713	1,300	1,713	1,713
GFEM	AEHF	2	2	1	2	2
Missile Defense	Patriot-MEADS CAP	718	646	500	700	646
Marine Air Group	H-1 Upgrades	218	218	218	218	218
Combat Aviation Brigade	AH-64E Remanufacture	431	300	200	300	300
Amphibious Ships	LHA 6	1	1	1	1	1
Missile Defense	SM-6	1,300	1,170	1,172	1,200	1,170
Naval Aviation	MQ-4C Triton	35	31	31	31	31
SSBN	Trident II	24	21	16	34	16

Note: The sum cost of the modernization profile for the Global Political-Economic-Military Competition strategic option is $25 billion less over the study period, in order to free up transfers out of DoD as noted above. The $25 billion figure comes out of a ramp-up over four years to $10 billion, with $2.5 billion, to $5 billion, to $7.5 billion, to $10 billion in subsequent years to enable capacity building inside the agencies for absorbing this increased funding.

- Force Structure/Weapons Implications (in contrast to the Baseline Option):
  - More: Surface combatants (LCS, DDG-51s) for global presence; Army light infantry and special operations (for indirect action); army aviation; theater lift (C-130Js); aerial ISR.
  - Less: Army heavy BCTs, attack subs, bombers, Air Force fighters, nuclear triad (fewer SSBS, Tridents), SSGNs.

<u>Step 5: Choose One of the Strategic Options as the 2021 Affordable Military</u>. The final step in the Affordable Military approach for coping with a deep defense drawdown is to choose one of the options as the recommended Affordable Military. If DoD were to adopt this methodological approach, there would be an exhaustive analysis of the costs and benefits of each alternative, including how well each did versus a range of defense planning scenarios and a detailed assessment of the risks associated with each option. For the purposes of this exercise, the CSIS study team made a number of judgments as it reached its recommendation that Option 3—Great Power Conflict—was the "least bad" option of the four.

Acceptance of the sequester-level budget caps forces difficult choices. Once the must-have capabilities are funded at 2012 levels or above (such as global ISR, the Marines as the nation's crisis-response force, and global counterterrorism) and plus-ups are added for a particular strategy (e.g., naval surface presence for the Asia-Pacific Rebalance), bill payers have to be found to offset the increases. Some force structure elements (e.g., carriers, SSBNs, and heavy BCTs) are very expensive, as are some weapon systems (e.g., attack subs and surface combatants). In comparison to the 2012 Pre-Drawdown Force, all of the 2021 options have capacity gaps.

- **Option 1**: As foreshadowed in the 2014 QDR's analysis of the impact of sequester-level cuts (see earlier discussion), the 2021 Baseline Force simply lacks the capacity to execute the portfolio approach to force planning. A comparison of the 2012 columns and the 2021 Baseline Force in Tables 3 and 4 reveal a dramatic loss of capacity across major elements of the 2012 Pre-Drawdown Force. Cuts range from over 50 percent (for heavy BCTs) to 18 percent (carriers). In our judgment, Secretary Robert Gates's goal for the 2010 QDR—that "the United States needs a broad portfolio of military capabilities with maximum versatility across the widest possible spectrum of conflict"—is no longer achievable in the FY 2021 fiscal environment.

- **Option 2**: Since the U.S. "pivot" to the Asia-Pacific was announced in late 2011, DoD has had difficulty convincing allies and partners in the region that the rebalance has been real. In part, this reflects the pressure of events, ranging from Syria to the domestic fiscal crisis to Ukraine, that demand the time of top-level officials (including the president) and prevent a greater focus on the Asia-Pacific. But there have also been capacity problems, which have prevented the United States from sending more assets to the region. This was already present with the Pre-Drawdown force structure that existed in 2012, not the 2021 force with its reduced capacities. Iraq and Afghanistan put great stress on the Army (both active and reserve) and, to a lesser extent, the Marines, but that does not explain why the Navy has found it harder to increase quickly its presence in the Asia-Pacific. The simplest explanation is the ongoing demands elsewhere around the globe, particularly in the Middle East. The United States is a global power with global interests. A regional policy, even one as important as the Asia-Pacific, is too difficult to execute.

- **Option 4**: Given the likely security environment of 2020+, the CSIS study team believes that the relatively benign security environment upon which the option of Global Political-Economic-Military Competition is predicated seems too optimistic. Setting aside (for the moment) U.S. relations with Russia and China, the current roster of international hot spots is daunting: Iran, Syria, and the Arab-Israeli conflict in the Middle East; India-Pakistan in South Asia; and Mali, South Sudan, and the Central African Republic in Africa. And although the security environment will undoubtedly change in the decade ahead, it is not likely to become less challenging. Moreover, the effectiveness of an increased reliance on "soft power"—including the four-year diversion of $25 billion from the defense budget—to address the underlying social and economic causes of political turmoil is far from clear. New sources of conflict, ranging from demographic trends to the effects of climate change, will add additional instability and chaos, increasing the likelihood that "soft power" means will, in the final analysis, be inadequate.

- **Option 3**: **The study team judged that an affordable military optimized for great power conflict was the most appropriate.** Recent events—such as China's more aggressive actions to secure its claims to 90 percent of the South China Sea and Russia's annexation of Crimea—certainly reinforce the idea that relations between the United States and its near-peer competitors seem more conflict prone. The U.S. ability to collaborate with Russia and China on shared security problems seems to be declining. Moreover, many U.S. allies, particularly in Europe, are engaged in their own defense drawdowns and seem less capable of contributing to their own defense. Inadequate burden sharing and "free riding" by U.S. allies has always been a problem for U.S. alliance management and seems likely to get worse as the United States copes with its own defense drawdown. In focusing its defense investments on the potential for greater conflict between the major powers, the United States is not preparing for a "war fight" with the China and Russia but pursuing its traditional "peace-through-strength" strategy for deterring, containing, and influencing its Cold War adversary. And by giving higher priority to capabilities that directly engage its powerful adversaries versus those aimed primarily at assuring U.S. friends and allies, the United States is sending the clear message, as the maxim goes, that "it will help those who help themselves." When establishing defense priorities during an age of austerity, DoD must look to its own interests first.

Choosing Option 3 as the recommended 2021 Affordable Military carries the risk of being a self-fulfilling prophecy, as an American foreign policy based on the assumption that China and Russia are competitors, not potential "strategic partners" or "responsible stakeholders," could cause the Chinese and Russians to act in the manner being assumed by a more assertive and nationalistic United States. In our judgment, the more accurate characterization is the exact opposite, namely, it has been China's rising assertiveness and Russia's increasingly anti-Western stance that is leading the United States to abandon its efforts to "shape" Russia's decline from its Cold War superpower status and the rise of China to great power status. The self-fulfilling prophecy belongs to China and Russia, as it is their behavior that leads us to conclude that the Great Power Conflict option is a prudent

---

"Cost-Capped" Methodology at a Glance

Although defense spending as a whole (base budget and OCO) peaked in FY 2010 (at $730 billion in 2013 dollars) when deployments in Afghanistan were at their highest, DoD's base budget peaked in FY 2012, and with OCO, totaled $660 billion in 2013 dollars. In FY 2021, under the budgetary caps imposed by the BCA of 2011, the budget will be $520 billion (again in 2013 dollars), which represents a decline of 21 percent. During this same time period, the defense dollar will have lost 15 percent of its purchasing power because of the aggregate impact of internal cost growth.

The "cost-capped" approach accepts this harsh fiscal reality as a given and attempts to maximize the military utility of a force that is affordable with significantly fewer resources through the following five steps:

1. Use the 2012 force structure as the Pre-Drawdown Force and cost it (both per unit and total) in FY 2021 dollars (as measured in constant 2013 dollars).

2. Applying the revised BCA caps and, using the BCA's across-the-board reduction (with the exception of military personnel), create the 2021 Sequester Force as default end point.

3. Build the 2021 Baseline Force by adapting the Sequester Force to 2020+ strategic realities (changes in the security environment and nature of warfare, plus sustain key competencies).

4. Create more strategic options (e.g., Asia-Pacific rebalance, Great Power Conflict and Global Political-Economic-Military competition in this exercise) by varying force structure within the cost caps.

5. Choose one of these options—the CSIS study team endorsed Great Power Conflict—as the 2021 Affordable Force.

The cost-capped approach is not very satisfying for strategists, who prefer to define a strategy that fits the strategic context and then ask "how much is enough?" In contrast, the cost-capped approach asks first "how much is affordable" and then develops alternative "strategies" for spending capped resources. Whether that is "enough" or sufficient for the strategic realities of 2020 and beyond is neither known nor assumed.

choice for the United States. The 2021 Affordable Military that is most likely to secure U.S. interests in an increasingly conflict-prone security environment is one that is optimized (within very rigid cost constraints) for great power conflict.

Final Thoughts

The 2021 fiscal reality facing DoD is a harsh one. DoD will have 21 percent fewer dollars with which to "buy" capabilities, and each of those dollars will have lost 15 percent of their purchasing power. The first step in reality-based force planning is acceptance: "It is what it is." The 2021 Sequester Force will comply with the budget caps mandated by the BCA, but it is not the "least bad" option. The 2021 Baseline Force, which has been adapted to the strategic realities of 2021 and beyond, is a better option than the 2021 Sequester Force but, in the judgment of the CSIS study team, it is still not the "least bad" option, in part because it still assumes the viability of the portfolio approach to force planning. The trend lines in the relationships between the United States and its near-peer competitors, China and Russia, are worsening—cooperation and competition have been largely replaced with competition, which itself is migrating toward conflict. While the CSIS study team agrees with the view of the current DoD leadership that sequester-level cuts will do irreparable damage to U.S. national security, we believe that the correct response is not denial and the continued submission of defense budget requests that do not conform to the Budget Control Act of 2011. Instead, we recommend that DoD embrace the cost-capped approach to coping with a deep defense drawdown and emulate the force planning approach taken in this report. We believe that a 2021 Affordable Military that is focused on the growing conflict with China and Russia is the "least bad" option for this punishing fiscal context of fewer and weaker defense dollars. More important, we believe that the cost-capped methodology and its 2021 cost calculators offers the Department of Defense a disciplined, practical approach to the consideration of alternative militaries, each designed to execute a different strategy, in times of severe constraints on DoD budgets. Different administrations will make different choices, but under this proposed methodology, each military will be affordable.

Appendix A. CSIS Affordable Military Working Group Participants

CSIS Study Team:

Clark Murdock, Chair*
Center for Strategic and International Studies

Ryan Crotty, Fellow*
Center for Strategic and International Studies

Lt. Col. Kevin Hickman, Air Force Fellow
Center for Strategic and International Studies

Angela Weaver, Research Assistant
Center for Strategic and International Studies

Working Group Participants:

Gordon Adams*
Stimson Center

David Berteau*
Center for Strategic and International Studies

Barry Blechman*
Stimson Center

Samuel Brannen
Center for Strategic and International Studies

Shawn Brimley
Center for a New American Security

Mackenzie Eaglen
American Enterprise Institute

Lou Finch*
Independent Consultant

Mike Fitzsimmons
Institute for Defense Analyses

Nathan Freier*
Center for Strategic and International Studies

Daniel Goure*
Lexington Institute

Rebecca Grant
IRIS Independent Research

Steven Grundman*
Atlantic Council

Scott Harris
Independent Consultant

Todd Harrison*
Center for Strategic and Budgetary Assessments

David Mosher
Congressional Budget Office

George "Chip" Pickett*
Independent Consultant

Russell Rumbaugh
Stimson Center

Kim Wincup*
Center for Strategic and International Studies

* Also a member of the CSIS Defense Drawdown Working Group (January–December 2012).

Appendix B. CSIS Defense Drawdown and Affordable Military Working Group Schedule

Defense Drawdown Working Group (DDWG)

Session 1: Overview of CSIS Approach and Assessment of DoD's Strategic Review

25 January 2012, 0800–0930, CSIS

DDWG will provide feedback on the Murdock-Wincup brief and discuss the 5 January DoD rollout of its adjusted strategy.

Session 2: Best Practices for Managing the Defense Drawdown

7 March 2012, 0830–1000, CSIS

DDWG will discuss a CSIS brief (lessons learned from past drawdowns and recommended design principles) and a commissioned brief on how DoD should address the management challenges facing them.

Session 3: Critical Factors Determining the Shape and Size of the Future Force

5 April 2012, 0800–1000, CSIS

DDWG will provide feedback to a CSIS brief and a commissioned brief that first identifies and then establishes priorities between the principal determinants for both defining the qualitative nature and the relative quantities of the capabilities needed by the 2020+ military.

Session 4: Interim Report Methodology and Future Security Environment

9 May 2012, 0800–1000, CSIS

DDWG will provide feedback on the CSIS interim report draft outline on how the defense drawdown should be conducted, receive a short brief on baselining the current drawdown, and discuss (if time permits) a CSIS brief on the context in which future military missions are likely to be executed.

Session 5: Must-Have Capabilities for the 2024 Force

18 July 2012, 0800–1000, CSIS

DDWG will discuss today's high-leverage capabilities and, based on the future security environment and likely evolution of warfare, identify additional "must-have" capabilities that will be required to cope with future challenges.

Session 6: A Revised Methodology for Preparing for a Deep Defense Drawdown

25 September 2012, 0800–1000, CSIS

DDWG will discuss the CSIS study team's revised methodological approach for how DoD should prepare for sequestration, an update of both the supply and demand functions of the methodology, and the "must-have" capabilities.

Session 7: Identifying the Common Core Capabilities and Building the 2021 Affordable Force

24 October 2012, 0800–1000, CSIS

DDWG will discuss CSIS and commissioned briefs that outline the minimal military capabilities needed to address the 2021 security challenges and solicit feedback on approaches to costing the 2021 Affordable Force.

Affordable Military Working Group (AMWG)

Session 1: Reconceptualizing the Defense Drawdown and Overview of the CSIS Approach

23 April 2013, 1200–1400, CSIS

AMWG will implement the cost-capped methodology for building an affordable future force that was developed through the DDWG in 2012 and intends to close the gap between ends and means as the Department of Defense copes with a shrinking topline and internal cost inflation.

Session 2: Institutional Support and Operational Forces

6 May 2013, 1200–1400, CSIS

AMWG will present and solicit feedback on the DDWG study team's preliminary breakdown of the DoD budget into "Institutional Support" and "Operational Forces."

Session 3: Costing Methodology for Force Structure Units

17 June 2013, CSIS

AMWG will provide an update on the CSIS study team's breakdown of institutional support and operational support and present the methodology for costing force structure units.

Session 4: The Future Security Environment and Common Core Capabilities

17 July 2013, 1200–1400, CSIS

AMWG will discuss and solicit feedback on the CSIS study team's assessment of the future security environment and the implications for the Common Core Capabilities.

Session 5: Building the Costed CSIS Force Structure

2 October 2013, 1200–1400, CSIS

AMWG will brief the CSIS study team methodology and results for breaking down the 2012 defense budget into "costed" force structure units and determining how much of the 2012 force structure DoD can afford in 2021.

Session 6: Developing the Common Core Capabilities

21 November 2013, 1200–1400, CSIS

AMWG will provide a briefing on the CSIS determination of how much of the 2012 force structure DoD can buy in 2021 and cover which of the Common Core Capabilities can be included within 35 percent and 50 percent of the budget.

Session 7: Minimum Essential Capabilities and the Strategic Trade Space

7 January 2014, 1200–1400, CSIS

AMWG will provide briefing on the CSIS study team's assessment of the Minimum Essential Capabilities for the 2021 force and look at the strategic options that can be implemented to augment the capacity and the capabilities within them.

Session 8: Working Group Wrap-Up and Final Feedback on the 2021 Affordable Force

11 February 2014, 1200–1400, CSIS

AMWG will provide briefing on the results of the study team's work, including the 2012 costed force, the 2021 Sequester force, and the 2021 reengineered force, as well as strategic options.

Appendix C. Evolution of the Methodology for Building the Affordable Military

Clark Murdock

The post-9/11 ramp-up in defense spending peaked in FY 2010 at $730 billion (in constant 2013 dollars), which includes both the base budget and all OCO funding. The BCA began the defense drawdown in earnest when it imposed budgetary caps on DoD totaling $487 billion over FY 2012– FY 2021. DoD responded quickly in September–December 2011 to this new fiscal reality by revisiting its defense strategy (as expressed in the February 2010 QDR report) in a process closely linked to its build of the FY 2013 budget request. In January 2012, the Department issued both a Defense Strategic Guidance and a white paper entitled "Defense Budget Priorities and Choices" that provided the fiscally constrained strategy for the FY 2013– FY 2017 Five-Year Defense Plan that implemented the BCA caps.

In late 2012, the likelihood of another round of defense budget cutbacks grew as the bipartisan "super committee" created by the BCA failed to reach an agreement in November 2012 on a debt reduction package of at least $1.2 trillion over 10 years. The BCA mandated that this failure would trigger sequester of the FY 2013 budget and a reduction of the BCA caps for FY 2013–FY 2021 to impose another approximately $1.2 trillion in cuts to discretionary defense and nondefense spending.[1] Although hope for avoiding these "devastating cuts" (as Secretary of Defense Leon Panetta frequently characterized them) flared briefly during the December 2012 "grand bargain" talks between the Obama administration and the House Republicans, the end-of-the-year deal that extended the Bush administration tax cuts (with a few exceptions) and passed an omnibus continuing resolution to fund the government through FY 2012 provided only limited relief from the BCA. For DoD, the "new normal" in defense spending had arrived. The traditional "guns vs. butter debate" had been replaced with two different national trade-offs—namely, "guns vs. increased taxes" and "guns vs. entitlements"—and defense appeared to be on the losing end of both debates.

---

1. Although the second round of BCA-mandated budget reductions are often referred to as the "sequester cuts," the only technical sequester so far has been to the FY 2013 budget (which was then being executed) as lower BCA caps were mandated for FY 2013–FY 2021 with the failure of the super committee. Breaching these new BCA caps, of course, would again trigger sequester.

Table C-1. Chronology of Key Developments and Events

2012

January	DoD releases 2012 DSG and "Defense Priorities and Choices." Applies first tranche of BCA caps FY 2012– FY 2107.
25 January	Defense Drawdown Working Group (DDWG) meets for first time.
7 March	At second DDWG meeting, CSIS study teams discusses "hollowing out" effect of internal cost growth on the defense budget.
5 April	Methodological focus on capabilities, not defense goals or national security objectives. Need to identify "must-have" capabilities, not portfolio of capabilities to cover widest possible range of contingencies.
May	DDWG Interim Report, "Planning for a Deep Defense Drawdown—Part 1: A Proposed Methodological Approach," released. Includes 7-step methodology.
July	CSIS study team recognized full impact of internal cost growth on the purchasing power of the defense dollar. Identifies macro-trade-off of modernization vs. personnel.
August	Changes topline projection from one-third real reduction in 2010–2024 to BCA caps (first and second tranche) for FY 2012–FY 2021.
25 September	Paradigm shifts from "Preparing for a Deep Drawdown" to "Building an Affordable Force." Vivid particular: restoring modernization (RDT&E, plus procurement) to historic 32 percent of the defense budget requires active-duty personnel cut of 661,000.
October	CSIS releases report by Murdock, Sayler, and Crotty, "The Defense Budget's Double Whammy: Drawing Down While Hollowing Out from Within."
12 November	DDWG reviews how budget is reconceptualized as Institutional Support and Operational Force.
18 December	Working draft of Common Core Capabilities reviewed at last meeting of the DDWG.

2013

8 February	At CSIS Military Strategy Forum, "Defense Budgeting to Beat the 'Double Whammy' " is presented.
March	Receives foundation grant to support Affordable Military study effort.
March	CBO publishes "Approaches for Scaling Back the Defense Department's Budget Plans."
23 April	First meeting of Affordable Military Working Group (AMWG).
6 May	AMWG reviews detailed breakdown of defense budget.
17 June	First review of CSIS methodology for costing 2021 capabilities.
17 July	Reviews draft list of Core Capabilities.
2 October	Reviews 2021 Cost Calculator (for force structure).

2014

7 January	AMWG reviews final characterization of "double whammy"—21 percent of budget shortfall due to topline reductions; 15 percent to internal cost growth.
11 February	Last meeting of AMWG. Discusses recent methodological adjustments and messaging.
March	Develops 2021 Modernization Cost Calculator.
April	Drafts final report and makes final adjustments to methodology.

Despite the somewhat histrionic rhetoric from senior DoD officials, the BCA Tranche 1 cuts ($487 billion over 10 years) and Tranche 2 cuts (subsequently $430 billion over nine years) constitute a relatively modest real decline in defense spending of 31 percent, still less than the post–Cold War drawdown of 36 percent, the post–Vietnam War drawdown of 33 percent, and the post–Korean War drawdown of 43 percent."[2] Convinced that DoD actually faced a succession of defense drawdowns because of the political gridlock over the federal deficit, CSIS senior advisers Clark Murdock and Kim Wincup convened a working group of former DoD officials and leading defense analysts to address the managerial challenges, including strategy and force structure implications, associated with a deep defense drawdown that was three to four times larger than the BCA-imposed reduction. The first meeting of the Defense Drawdown Working Group (DDWG) was held on 25 January 2012.[3]

The methodology for building the Affordable Military was largely developed during the 2012 DDWG process, although important innovations (such as the 2021 Force Cost Calculator) were made during 2013. This appendix tracing the evolution of the Affordable Military methodology is provided for several reasons:

- To make as explicit and as transparent as possible the many underlying assumptions and causal relationships contained in the Affordable Military methodology;

- To trace the development of a deeper understanding of the true magnitude of the budgetary challenge facing DoD in the next decade;

- To contribute to the development of a new approach to formulating defense strategy under severe budget constraints in an effort to move beyond the increasingly sterile debate between "strategy-driven" and "budget-driven" processes.[4]

The development of the Affordable Military methodology has been a fascinating and fruitful process of discovery to which many have contributed. Of most importance have been the study team's current members, Clark Murdock, Ryan Crotty, and Angela Weaver; and former members, Vince Manzo, Eric Ridge, and Kelley Sayler. Many members of the Defense Drawdown Working Group and the Affordable Military Working Group (AMWG) have made significant contributions, but special thanks are owed to those who participated in both working groups (see Appendix A). I am particularly indebted to my DDWG cochair, Kim Wincup, for his wise and pragmatic counsel. This two-year-plus study effort has been

---

2. CSIS analysis of data from Office of the Secretary of Defense (Comptroller), *National Defense Budget Estimates for FY 2013*, Washington, D.C.: Department of Defense, March 2012.

3. Clark Murdock was the project director of a CSIS team that held the September 29, 2011, conference "Defense in an Age of Austerity" and issued a conference report in October 2011. See Clark A. Murdock, Kelley Sayler, and Kevin Kallmyer, "Defense in an Age of Austerity: Conference Proceedings, Presentations, and Key Takeaways," Center for Strategic and International Studies, October 2011, http://csis.org/files/publication /222221_Murdock_DefenseAusterity_Web.pdf. Although the period of performance on that contract ended in mid-November 2021 with all of its tasks completed, the DDWG effort represented "follow-on work" to that conference and fulfills a handshake commitment made by the project director.

4. In response to House Armed Services Committee Chairman Buck McKeon's charge that the 2014 QDR report was "budget-driven, shortsighted and assumes too much risk," Deputy Assistant Secretary of Defense David Ochmanek said on March 18, 2014: "I would take issue with that. We were resource-informed but we were strategy driven." *Inside the Pentagon* (March 20, 2014), 16.

one of the most enjoyable, interesting, and productive efforts of my professional career and, in my view, warranted this detailed knowledge-capturing exercise, if only to give thanks to those who have so generously given their time to this effort.

At the Outset, a Process but Not an Analytic Methodology

The DDWG cochairs believed strongly that it was critically important to establish long-range defense priorities for a deep defense drawdown so that today's budgetary cuts could be guided by longer-term realities and priorities. The 25 January 2012 DDWG methodological approach stated the following as one of its *"underlying policy assumptions"*: [NOTE: *Italics* indicate material from past DDWG/AMWG documents produced by the CSIS study team.]

- *Decisions made during the first round of budget cuts should be informed by the longer-term strategic, capability, and organizational consequences of even steeper reductions in defense spending.*
  - *Knowing what is core—with respect to interests, strategy, or capabilities—and what is less essential or important prevents one from taking actions today that foreclose or constrain future options that are critical.*
    - *There are also actions that must be taken today to ensure that critical options will be available in the future.*

This short handout also stated the DDWG's *"operational philosophy"*:

- *In the final analysis, making hard choices comes down to judgment. And it is the judgment of experienced people that matters the most.*
  - *Charles Cook: "Experience is not an end in itself. It's a means to an end; the end is judgment."*
  - *On what is needed for making tough choices, John Hillen: "Good judgment learned through hard experience."*
  - *DDWG consists of some very smart people and some very experienced former practitioners [note: these are not mutually exclusive groupings] whose interactions offer the best chance (but only that) for sound analysis and recommendations.*
- *The competition of ideas is critical.*
  - *Many ideas are generated in solitude, but they evolve and are forged through healthy and rigorous debate.*
  - *The quality of any debate depends on the trust and confidence of the participants that it is the ideas that are being discussed, not personalities and political agendas.*

Reliance on experienced judgment and the competition of ideas has remained central to this two-year-plus study effort.

The substantive content of the DDWG approach was reflected in its meeting agenda:

Session 1: Overview of CSIS Approach & DoD's January 2012 Strategic Guidance (25 January 2012)

    a) DDWG Methodological Approach—Clark Murdock

    b) Comparison of Defense Drawdowns—Ryan Crotty (CSIS)

    c) Overview of new Strategic Guidance—Kelley Sayler (CSIS)

    d) Scorecard of DoD post-Guidance budgetary actions[5]—Sayler & Crotty

Session 2: Best Practices for Managing the Defense Drawdown (7 March 2012)

    a) Best practices from the private sector—Steven Grundman [independent consultant now associated with the Atlantic Council]

    b) Lessons learned from previous defense drawdowns—Kelley Sayler

    c) Obama administration's lessons from past drawdowns—Clark Murdock

    d) Scoping the drawdown—Ryan Crotty

Session 3: Critical Factors Determining the Shape and Size of the Future Force (3 April 2012)

    a) Scenario Four: Major Strategic Redefinition—George "Chip" Pickett, Independent Corporation

    b) Application of the Net Assessment Methodology—John Milam and Bud Hays

    c) CSIS Study Group—Clark Murdock

Session 4: Sustaining a High-Quality All Volunteer Force (9 May 2012)

Session 5: Maintaining the U.S. Technological Edge (13 June 2012)

Final Session: CSIS Findings and Recommendations (TBD)

The DDWG stayed on this path for the first two sessions, but Murdock started almost immediately (31 January 2012) to re-scope the DDWG study effort and to develop a new methodology that was tabled at the April meeting (along with alternatives approaches from Pickett and Milam and Hays). At the March meeting, however, Ryan Crotty brought to the DDWG's attention the CSIS study team's growing awareness of how much internal cost inflation was "hollowing out" the defense budget from within. Sparked by a comment made at the 25 January session by the Center for Strategic and Budgetary Assessments's Todd Harrison,[6] one of the policy community's top defense budget analysts,

---

5. Ryan Crotty and Kelly Sayler, *DDWG Defense Budget Tracker* (Washington, D.C.: Center for Strategic and International Studies, February 14, 2012), http://csis.org/files/120126_DDWG_Defense_Budget_Tracker.pdf.

6. Todd Harrison, *Analysis of the FY2012 Defense Budget* (Washington, D.C.: Center for Strategic and Budgetary Assessments, July 14, 2011), http://www.csbaonline.org/publications/2011/07/analysis-of-fy2012-defense.budget/. In his analysis, Harrison characterized the post-9/11 doubling of the defense budget as one of "hollow growth":

Overall, nearly half of the growth in defense spending over the past decade is unrelated to the wars in Afghanistan and Iraq—personnel costs grew while end strength remained relatively flat, the cost of peacetime operations grew while the pace of peacetime operations declined, and acquisition costs increased while the inventory of equipment grew smaller and older. The base budget now supports a force with essentially the same size, force structure, and capabilities as in FY2001 but at a 35 percent higher cost. The Department is spending more but not getting more.

Figure C-1. The Effect of Military Pay and Benefits

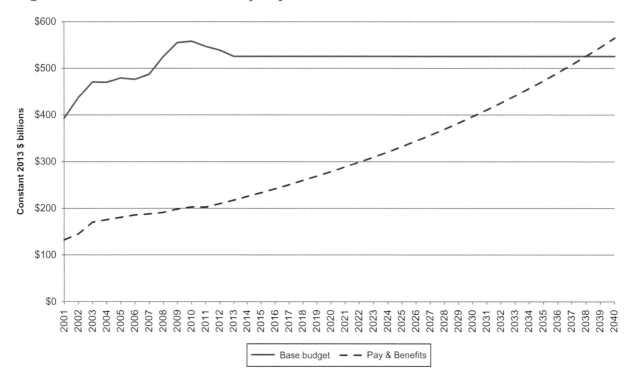

Concept for figure courtesy of Todd Harrison.
Sources: Department of Defense FY 2013 Budget Overview Book; FY 2000–FY 2012 Green Books; FY 2000–FY 2012 Defense Health Program Justification Books.
Note: "Military Pay and Benefits" was calculated by summing the Military Personnel account, the Defense Health Program, and Medicare-Eligible Retired Healthcare Fund. Beyond 2012, pay and benefits were calculated at a growth rate equal to that from 2001 to 2012.

Figure C-1 portrays how military pay and benefits, if they continued at the current rate of growth, which Secretary Panetta often characterized as "unsustainable," would consume the entire FY 2012 defense base budget (if it remained constant in real dollars) in 2038. As will be documented in this appendix, the cumulative impact of internal cost inflation across DoD's major functions (that is, personnel pay and benefits; operation and maintenance, or O&M; and acquisition) exceeds that of the declining defense budget on DoD's future military capacity.

Growing Resource Constraints Cause Greater Emphasis upon Key Capabilities

As one of its boundary assumptions for implementing a deep defense drawdown, the 5 April 2012 CSIS paper "Shaping and Sizing the 2024 Force"[7] put its focus on *"military capabilities and the ability to execute missions assigned to the military, not on meeting defense goals or national security objectives."* Using defense goals, such as promoting stability in

---

7. At this time, the planning time frame was 15 years, the approximate time needed to develop and field a new capability, and the start date for the projected defense drawdown was 2010, the peak year of the post-9/11 buildup. Subsequently, the CSIS study team decided to use the period covered by the BCA, since it imposed mandatory budget caps for FY 2012 through FY 2022.

Northeast Asia or responsibly ending wars in Iraq and Afghanistan, as a tool for shaping and sizing the force is not very useful, because so many analytic judgments are required to assess the extent to which a particular set of capabilities achieves a higher-level defense goal. In a similar vein, the 2012 DSG objective, as stated by Chairman of the Joint Chiefs of Staff General Martin Dempsey, of "retaining capability across the full spectrum of conflict"[8] both fails to set priorities, which is necessary during a deep defense drawdown, and runs the risk of spreading a finite amount of military capabilities too thinly across a robust set of contingencies. This boundary assumption led directly to the first recommended design principle for the defense drawdown—namely, *"Adjust strategy to deep budget cuts by aligning ends to means and shedding missions."* This reflected the study leader's conviction that the *"pursuit of ambitious goals with inadequate means is a recipe for disaster."* During an era of defense austerity, the key to ensuring that the capabilities at hand are sufficient to get the mission accomplished is to scale back the missions being sought until they can be achieved with the capabilities the nation can afford.

In the first of its sequential-steps methodologies for conducting a defense drawdown, the 3 April 2012 paper recommended the following (emphasis and some sub-bullets removed from the original):

1. Identify today's high-leverage capabilities that will still be relevant to 2024 military operations and ensure that these capabilities will be sustained and defended against direct and indirect attacks.

2. Based upon one's best understanding of the future security environment (both in 2024 and beyond) and the likely evolution of warfare, identify those additional (to those identified in Step 1) military capabilities that a future Joint Force Commander "must have" to cope with future challenges.
   a. Developing new capabilities to address "critical future deficiencies" and then defending and sustaining them, completes the 2024 portfolio of critical military capabilities that comprise the Desired 2024 Force.

3. As an external check to this deductive approach for defining the Desired 2024 Force, assess how well this draft portfolio of capabilities stacks up against alternative definitions of the demand for military capabilities, whether defined by missions (the 200X Joint Operational Concept), priorities (the "five P's" of the 2010 QDR) or defense goals (Michael O'Hanlon's The Wounded Giant), and make necessary judgments.

4. Leverage existing U.S. strengths (high rate of defense expenditures, ability to weaponize technology, etc.) by forcing the pace of military innovation through a robust level of S&T and R&D investment.
   a. Although the U.S. defense budget has started to decline, the U.S. still . . . accounts for half of total global R&D expenditures. Aggressively exploring what is "militarily

---

8. Martin Dempsey, *The Future of U.S. Landpower: Special Operations Versatility, Marine Corps Utility* (Washington, D.C.: National Defense University, 2013), 85, https://www.mca-marines.org/files/JFQ-69_84-91 _Stringer-Sizemore.pdf.

doable" in areas of advancing technology is the United States' asymmetric advantage over the rest of the world and a key component of its military superiority.

5. The first step in sizing the 2024 force is to determine the targeted endpoint of a 2024 force that costs about one-third less (in real terms) than the 2010 force (the peak of the post-9/11 buildup) in terms of its "adjusted base budget."

6. Using rough order of magnitude (ROM) cost estimates of 2024 capability components, build the Desired 2024 Force consisting of the following elements: (1) the "institutional force" at 30% of Total Obligational Authority (TOA) which supports (from recruiting to the service academies) the operational force; (2) the "innovation account" which consists of 2% of TOA for S&T, X% of TOA for RDT&E and Y% of TOA for procurement; and (3) the "operational force," which consists of the force structure (and end-strength) that actually conducts military operations.

    a. Knowing what you would buy (the Desired 2024 Force) if you could afford it is a critical departure point for starting the iterative prioritization process.

7. Develop alternative paths, each representing different strategies and priorities, for moving from the Desired 2024 Force to the Affordable 2024 Force, identify the implications of each path, and make a recommendation on which one to follow.

    a. Deciding which capability to give up first reverses the more common bottom-up approach that begins by identifying the most important capability and "building up" to the Affordable 2024 Force.

        i. It is both analytically easier, since it avoids having to prioritize between those capabilities that are going "to make the cut" in any case, and politically and bureaucratically easier, since the "winners" have all been identified up front and will coalesce against the lower-priority "losers" (see the BRAC process).

Several features of this first DDWG methodological process for a deep drawdown (defined as a defense budget about one-third less in real terms) are particularly noteworthy:

- The departure point is defining the future forces' key capabilities,[9] which consist of both current capabilities sustained into the future and new capabilities developed to address future challenges.

- Shaping the force is deciding what kinds of capabilities are needed; sizing the force is determining how much of each kind of capability is required. During a deep defense drawdown, the risk incurred by seeking a "full-spectrum force," which is

---

9. This author prefers the term "key capabilities" or "critical capabilities" to "core competencies," because of their external focus—that is, they are the capabilities critical to meeting the security environment's demands or key to dominating a domain of warfare. The term "core competency" has an internal focus, because it emphasizes sustaining a capability that a firm, organization, or a nation may have. Ideally, one wants to have a core competency that addresses the demand function, but all too often (see the U.S. Army and the horse cavalry and IBM and the mainframe computer at the beginning of the PC era) the internal focus of core competencies can lead an organization to focus on what it likes to do, not what it needs to do.

the natural inclination of military planners who plan for the widest possible range of contingencies, is having insufficient capacity for important missions.

- The process conceptualizes the defense budget as consisting of the "institutional force," that portion of DoD that supports (from recruiting to the service academies) the "operational force,"[10] which consists of the force structure that actually conducts military operations, and the "innovation account," which subsequently becomes "modernization" (consisting of RDT&E plus procurement).

- Estimates were developed for what capabilities would cost in 2024, not 2012, since internal cost inflation was weakening the purchasing power of the defense dollar in terms of how much capacity could be provided per dollar.

- Choices about which strategy to follow in 2024 were to be expressed by "alternative paths, each representing different strategies and priorities." From this menu of alternative paths, which subsequently became a "set of strategic options," one path would be chosen and anointed "the Affordable 2024 Force."

The DDWG cochairs also proposed that they (not the working group itself) would produce an interim report (to be released in May) to provide timely advice to "[h]elp DoD think through how a deeper defense drawdown should be conducted and provide a set of recommendations on what decisions the Department should make."[11] To reflect the significant evolution of its methodological approach, the cochairs also revised the meeting agenda for 2012:

- *Session 4: Interim Report Methodology & Future Security Environment (9 May)*

- *Session 5: Must-Have Capabilities for the 2024 Force (18 July)*

- *Session 6: CSBS Portfolio Rebalancing Exercise[12] (12 August)*

- *Session 7: Costing the 2024 Force (25 September)*

- *Session 8: Roster of Alternative 2024 Force Mixes (24 October)*

Following an intense, extremely useful discussion at the 5 April 2012 DDWG meeting, Murdock converted his 3 April paper into an extended outline of the interim report and edited it several times within CSIS before tabling it with the DDWG at the 9 May 2012

---

10. Note the use of the term "operational force" rather than "fighting force." Today's military conducts many missions that are not "fighting" or combat missions. The much-abused use of the term "warfighter" often obscures differentiating between those in DoD who actually execute missions and those who support them.

11. Clark A. Murdock, Ryan A. Crotty, and Kelley Sayler, *Planning for a Deep Defense Drawdown—Part 1: A Proposed Methodological Approach* (Washington, D.C.: Center for Strategic and International Studies, May 2012).

12. In part to reflect the DDWG cochairs' appreciation for Todd Harrison's fulsome participation in the DDWG effort, they agreed to use the DDWG as a forum for the Center for Strategic and Budgetary Assessments exercise on how to rebalance DoD's portfolio of capabilities as it implemented (in two moves) the BCA "sequester cuts." This exercise was very useful in its own right and reinforced Murdock's conviction about two design principles for a deep defense drawdown: (1) determine first what the desired capabilities of the future force are and make the necessary "adds" before starting the "cut drill"; and (2) when implementing reductions in force structure (and end strength), make them as quickly as possible in order to reap full savings from the reductions and to keep the defense budget topline from declining even further.

meeting. The number of steps in the sequential methodology went from seven to eight and then back to seven again as several significant changes were made:

- A demand-supply paradigm in which *"DoD supplies forces to meet the demand for military capabilities,"* although it was noted that in the defense arena supply never meets demand:

  - *Unlike the market place, where the cost of a product reflects where supply meets demand, the demand for military capabilities (no nation ever is completely secure) always exceeds supply. How much a nation is willing to pay for defense—that is, the defense budget—determines how much of the demand for military capabilities it is willing to meet. During an era of declining budgets, the "gap" between demand and supply grows and puts a higher premium on price (see Cost as an Independent Variable or CAIV) in the drive to find a more affordable way of acquiring military capabilities.*

- Adding the demand-supply paradigm, however, created a new first step to the methodology, one that puts the identification of key capabilities into an external, demand-driven context:

  - *Step 1: "Paint a picture" of the multi-dimensional demand for military capabilities that provides a framework and context for making tough trade-off decisions needed to prioritize U.S. defense capabilities.*

  - *The judgment of senior-level decision makers (both civilian and military) will be critical in deciding which drivers are the most important determinants of the demand function and which portfolio of capabilities best meets that demand. Providing a holistic context that identifies what is known about the future security environment, as well as the endemic uncertainty of the "known unknowns" and the "unknown unknowns" (to use Secretary Rumsfeld's now-classic formulation) will help inform their judgment and better enable them to manage the risk associated with future-oriented, cost-constrained strategic choices.*[13]

- The boundary assumption that *"no further gains from increased efficiency are assumed"* was softened slightly by adding *"although continuing improvements in how the Pentagon does business are most desirable because they free up resources to buy more capability."*

  - Prior to 5 January 2012, DoD had identified more than $150 billion in savings over five years due to efficiency initiatives. On 5 January 2012, when it released the 2012 DSG, the Department claimed another $60 billion in new projected savings over FY 2013–FY 2017. While recognizing the importance of increasing DoD's efficiency, the real opportunity costs of inefficiency are not just "wasted dollars" but unacquired capabilities that could have improved the security of the American people.[14]

---

13. Murdock, Crotty, and Sayler, *Planning for a Deep Defense Drawdown*, 1.

14. Despite its uneven (at best) record of actually realizing these projected savings, DoD keeps projecting additional savings from efficiencies in order to make the numbers work: the FY 2015 budget request adds another $129 billion on top of the prior projections of $210 billion. In the author's view, this just stacks another

- Despite skepticism about achieving the claimed $200 billion-plus in efficiency savings, the onset of a deep defense drawdown makes it imperative that DoD become more efficient in how it uses increasingly scarce defense dollars. This led the CSIS team to add the "cost-capped" approach to generating defense savings to its methodology later in October.

- Perhaps the most important input from the 5 April DDWG meeting was made by someone who was unable to attend but had reviewed the three presentations (by Pickett, Milam/Hays, and Murdock) carefully: *"Of the three presentations, yours is the only one that gets into the space of real tradeoffs. As you point out, the only way to size the force is to iterate between desired capabilities and available resources. You offer a solid framework for doing so. Good costing will be essential."*

  - This observation was welcomed, because it suggested that the DDWG analytic methodology was gaining maturity and increasing acceptance as a "solid framework." But it also raised a daunting task—that is, building a credible costing tool for future capabilities. The effort to do this took well over a year.

At the same time that DDWG methodology for how DoD should conduct a deep defense drawdown evolved, the justification for why DoD needed to adopt the recommended approach matured as well and became more compelling.

The Origins of the "Double Whammy" Narrative

On 8 February 2013, Murdock gave a brief entitled "Defense Budgeting to Beat the 'Double Whammy'" at the CSIS Military Strategy Forum "Preparing for a Deep Defense Drawdown." In response to the positive reaction to the webcasted event and based on the event transcript, Murdock and Crotty subsequently published a monograph[15] that went through two publication runs. This monograph began by describing the budgetary *"double whammy"* that DoD faced:

> The president, civilian and military defense leaders, and some members of the Congress have spent the last year-and-a half decrying the effects of budget cuts on the Department of Defense (DoD). Yet, topline reductions are only the first piece of the "double whammy" that defense faces today. Equally serious, the defense dollar has lost—and continues to lose—its purchasing power due to the aggregate impact of internal cost growth, for personnel, for operations and maintenance, and for acquisition programs. It is this second trend, on top of the budget cuts, that has driven the Defense Department to react so strongly to a sequester that, on the surface, looks like just an 8 to 10 percent cut. But it is going to feel much deeper, because it comes on top

---

unachievable "negative funding wedge" on top of another. See page 5 of the comptroller's budget briefing here: http://comptroller.defense.gov/Portals/45/Documents/defbudget/fy2015/fy2015_Budget_Request.pdf.

15. Clark A. Murdock and Ryan A. Crotty, *A Methodology for Making the Right Trade-offs in Defense for the Decade Ahead: Defense Budgeting to Beat the "Double Whammy"* (Washington, D.C.: Center for Strategic and International Studies, 2013), http://csis.org/files/publication/130417_Murdock_DefenseBudgetingDoubleWhammy_Web.pdf.

of another 8 to 10 percent cut (caused by the first set of budget caps imposed by the Budget Control Act of 2011), and, at the same time, it is being hollowed out from within by internal cost growth. That is why a 20 percent reduction in the defense budget is going to feel a lot more like a 40 percent reduction.

This "double whammy" metaphor has proved to be quite powerful,[16] but like the methodology it supports, it took time for it to evolve. Unlike the defense drawdown methodology, which was developed primarily through the interaction between the CSIS study team and its working groups (the DDWG during 2012 and the AMWG during 2013), the "double whammy" narrative emerged from iterations within the CSIS study team as they sought to portray the budgetary challenges facing DoD in a compelling manner. This pursuit of what came to be called the "oh-my!" charts—the reaction of one senior Pentagon official in late 2012 to a chart that portrayed how much of the Pentagon's budget was consumed by internal cost growth by 2021)—sharpened the team's analysis considerably.

The narrative began in the comparison of the current defense drawdown to previous ones (see Figure C-2). In order to do the comparison, we included both the base budget and spending for OCO and other such supplemental funding because DoD had never systematically separated spending for military operations from the rest of defense spending.[17] The point being made in Figure C-2 (which we started using in early 2012) was that past drawdowns had averaged 35 percent, but the current drawdown, which at the time included only the first $487 billion mandated by the BCA, was a very modest seven to eight percent, even though defense spending had ballooned by almost 75 percent between 2001 and 2010.

As portrayed in Figure C-3, a chart that we first started using in January 2012, we superimposed the yearly data on active-duty troop levels on what was spent each year on defense.

When briefing Figure C-3, we would point out that the post-9/11 buildup was very different from that for Korea or Vietnam, because increased spending did not pay for more active-duty troops but instead went largely for civilian employees and contractors as well as active-duty pay for mobilized reservists and Guard troops. We also started to make the

---

16. The American Enterprise Institute's Mackenzie Eaglen reported in early March 2014 that she had added a "third whammy": Congress rejects all proposals, even the ones that it makes itself (the cost-saving measure in the Bipartisan Budget Act of January 2014 that imposed a one percent reduction in the COLA increase to the retirement benefits of uniformed personnel who are of working age), to address the internal cost growth problem.

17. In both the Korean War (1951) and the Vietnam War (in 1966 and 1967), DoD paid for the wars through supplemental appropriations, but in both cases, war spending was quickly folded back into the base budget. This was not the case for the wars in Afghanistan and Iraq, primarily for two reasons: (1) since OCO (initially called "the supplementals") was outside of the normal budget process and was not "scored" against deficit reduction packages, it was politically easier to vote for war funding for the troops than it is for general discretionary spending; and (2) OCO appropriations have frequently been used as slush funds for underfunded items in military spending. The "OCO-to-base" problem—that is, paying for procurement and O&M that will eventually be covered by the base budget (when "normal" spending practices are restored)—is estimated at anywhere between $10 and $20 billion annually. FY 2008 saw the largest supplemental appropriation at $187 billion, about 30 percent of the defense budget. From FY 2001 through FY 2012, over $1.3 trillion was spent in the supplemental/OCO accounts.

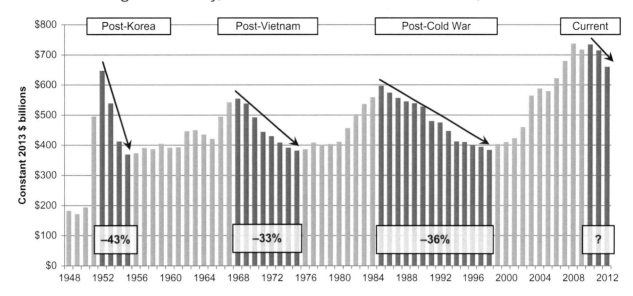

Figure C-2. Defense Drawdowns since World War II
Total DoD Budget Authority, in billions of constant 2013 dollars, 1948–2012

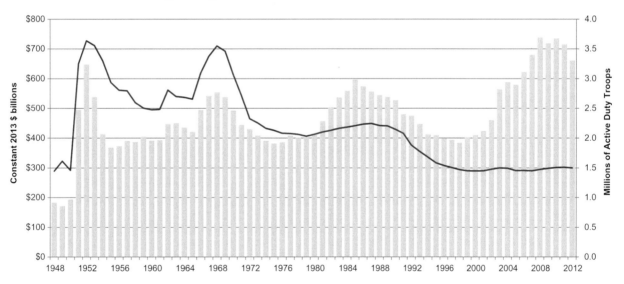

Figure C-3. Defense Budget and Active-Duty Troop Levels, 1948–2012
Total DoD Budget Authority, in billions of constant 2013 dollars, and
millions of active-duty troops

broader argument that the framework for looking at trade-offs between personnel, modernization, and readiness during the coming defense drawdown was not just the declining defense drawdown (as portrayed in Figures C-2 and C-3) but also *the internal pressure from the rising cost of doing business within the Department*":

> These internal constraints are generated by the inflation of costs within the
> defense budget over the past decade. The increasing costs of doing business that do
> not correspond to an increase in capability have led to a weakening defense dollar,

where each dollar in the defense budget buys less than it did the year before. The cumulative effect of this weak defense dollar is a "hollowing out from within."

Similarly, cost growth in internal accounts, including personnel and operations and maintenance, projects to continue in the future, and this will in turn crowd out other areas of discretionary spending.[18]

Although our quantitative analysis would deepen and our portrayal of the "double whammy" effect of top-down and internal pressure on the defense budget would become more vivid, the basic argument for why this defense drawdown was different was developed quite quickly.

The DDWG Methodology at Midpoint: The Seven-Step Approach

At its 9 May 2012 meeting, the CSIS study team tabled its revised methodological approach and the charts that it planned to include in its interim report. Following another fruitful discussion, the CSIS study team revised its methodology and released its interim report on 24 May in a seven-step version that incorporated the demand-supply paradigm:

Step 1: "Paint a picture" of the multi-dimensional demand for military capabilities that provides a framework and context for making the tough trade-off decisions needed to prioritize U.S. defense capabilities.

Step 2: Identify today's high-leverage capabilities that will still be relevant to 2024 military operations and ensure that these capabilities will be sustained and defended against direct and indirect attacks.

Step 3: Based upon one's best understanding of the future demand for military capability (see Step 1), identify those military capabilities (additional to those identified in Step 2) that a Joint Force Commander "must have" to cope with future challenges.

Step 4: The first step in sizing the 2024 force is to determine the targeted endpoint of a deeper defense drawdown force that costs about one-third less in real terms) than the total cost (both base budget and "war funding") of the 2010 force, the point at which the post-9/11 buildup peaked.

Step 5: Build a template for the 2024 force that consists of at least the following components:[19]

---

18. Ryan A. Crotty, "Appendix B: Baselining the Current Defense Drawdown," in Murdock, Crotty, and Sayler, *Preparing for a Deep Defense Drawdown*, 36–37.

19. If it were politically doable, DoD should deliberately plan for uncertainty and set aside a portion (perhaps two percent) of its TOA in an "Unpredictability Reserve" that would provide resources that hedges against uncertainty and would enable the Pentagon to respond quickly to unforeseen developments and events. This would function much like the "management reserve" of acquisition programs in the private sector that are premised on the knowledge that any acquisition program will encounter unexpected cost, schedule, and performance difficulties. However, long-standing Congressional hostility to contingency funds and their

- Capability Tradespace: the percent (TBD) of TOA that is available for acquiring and sustaining equipment, personnel and infrastructure and comprises the "operational force."
- Innovation account: the percent (perhaps 11% for RDT&E, including 2.5% for basic S&T, and 20% for procurement) which enables the [United States] to force the pace of military innovation, shape the evolution of warfare, and maintain its technological superiority; creating "strategic surprise" by fielding capabilities developed in black programs (e.g. precision strike in the 1970s, stealth in the 1980s and, perhaps, directed energy in the 2020s) [that] can be a game-changer.
- Institutional force: the percentage (perhaps 30% as a stretch goal) of TOA that supports (for the Title 10 responsibilities of the military services, policy development, and oversight functions of OSD and the JS, the Combatant Command structures, etc.) the operational force.

Step 6: Build rough order of magnitude (ROM) cost estimates of the specific 2024 capabilities (to include weapons, force structure units, and associated infrastructure) in the capability portfolios.

Step 7: Using the 2024 capability portfolios developed in Steps 2 and 3, and the inventory of costing profiles built in Step 6, develop a roster of 4–5 alternative 2024 force mixes for the $XX billion (TBD) available for capability tradeoffs (see Step 5), each representing different strategies and priorities for how DoD should spend its scarce operational capability dollars in 2024.[20]

In addition to embracing the demand-supply framework, sustaining the focus on capabilities, and assuming a one-third reduction of the defense budget, the DDWG methodology had started its reconceptualization of the defense budget by breaking out the "institutional force." This is the relatively fixed portion of DoD activities (largely resident in the military services) that are needed to support any mixture of military capabilities. It should also be noted that strategy issues are not addressed "up front" in the process (as is implied by the phrase "strategy-driven process") but are left to the end, where they are expressed as choices between different mixes of capabilities. Finally, the CSIS study team underscored (or "foot stomped" in Pentagonese) the importance of *a credible process for estimating the costs of future capabilities*:

> During the summer of 2012, the CSIS study team will either develop a credible process for future capability costing or, failing that, come up with a less good way of informing these critical force development decisions. There is only one certainty, namely that these decisions will be made, either explicitly or implicitly. Our preference is for a deliberate planning process where the decisions are made explicitly in a transparent manner that invites debate.[21]

"undefined dollars" (that is, dollars not attached to specific purposes) makes this possible recommendation a non-starter. [*Note: This footnote was in the original draft.*]

20. Murdock, Crotty, and Sayler, *Preparing for a Deep Defense Drawdown*, 21–26.

21. Ibid., 25.

People and weapons will cost more in 2021 than they do in 2012. And DoD will have fewer dollars to buy them. Capacity shortfalls may be the biggest challenge.

Identifying the Big Trade-off: Personnel versus Modernization

At the 12 July 2012 DDWG meeting, the CSIS study team addressed Steps 1, 2, and 4 of the May 2012 methodology and made progress in "painting a picture" of the 2014 security environment and identifying key capabilities in the current force that would need to be sustained into 2020 and beyond (these issues will be addressed shortly). What became dramatically clear by the July meeting was that the internal cost growth challenge to DoD was far greater than initially anticipated. As mentioned previously, we were using a projected topline budget reduction that would consist of a one-third real decline in the budget from 2010 (the peak of the post-9/11 buildup) to 2024 (with no funds for OCO). As portrayed in Figure C-4, the rising cost of personnel, the Defense Health Program (both of which had been adjusted for planned personnel reductions), and O&M had "crowded out" all spending for modernization. In 2010, 35 percent of the budget, or $258 billion in 2013 dollars, had been spent on modernization (RDT&E and procurement); in 2024, there were no funds available for modernization as spending on pay, benefits, and O&M exceeded the total budget by three percent ($14 billion). And this was the best case. If the high end of internal growth rate estimates (for pay, benefits, and O&M) were used and acquisition cost growth (at 2.3 percent per year) was factored in, the available space for modernization was a *negative* 22 percent ($109 billion in 2013 dollars). These dramatic results caused the CSIS

Figure C-4. Operation and Support vs. CSIS Topline Projection
High end of growth rate estimates + 2.3 percent acquisition cost growth

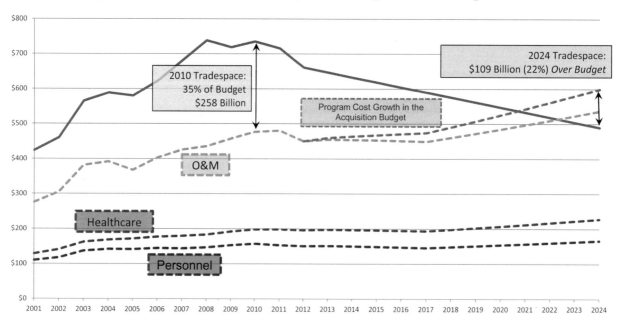

team to both start examining more dramatic options for restoring modernization spending and to go back and double-check the analysis that had brought them to this preliminary conclusion.

At the 18 July 2012 DDWG meeting, the CSIS team tabled its first step in addressing the macro-trade-off between modernization and personnel end strength when it estimated that the effect of removing 100,000 troops in the period of 2017–2024 would result in $147 billion (in 2013 dollars) in savings. Using the conservative estimates for internal cost growth (and not including acquisition cost growth), cutting 100,000 personnel (over the period of 2017–2024) would result in about $38 billion in savings and allow the tradespace for modernization to be increased from negative three percent to five percent of the budget. Of course, this was far short of the 35 percent of the budget ($258 billion in 2013 dollars) spent on modernization in 2010, but it was a start.

As part of its revalidation of the "double whammy" analysis, the CSIS study team de-cided to abandon the "CSIS Topline Projection" (of a 2010–2024 real budget decline of one-third) and embrace the reductions mandated by the BCA and the assumptions made about OCO by the Congressional Budget Office (CBO), which is widely regarded as the most author-itative source of budgetary analysis in the Washington policy community. Adopting the BCA caps meant shortening the time frame of our analysis from FY 2010–FY 2024 (which started at the peak of the post-9/11 buildup) to FY 2012–FY 2021; the first tranche of BCA caps totaled $487 billion over 10 years; the second tranche, which would be triggered in January 2013 if Congress failed to reach a "grand bargain" deficit-reduction deal, would total $492 billion over nine years.[22] While this change made our analysis of the current drawdown less comparable to previous drawdowns (since it no longer includes funding for overseas operations), it strengthened the credibility of our depiction because we relied on what was mandated in law and on assumptions made by respected institutions. As ex-plained in Appendix D and portrayed in Table C-2, we followed the same approach in firming up our estimates of internal cost growth for O&M (relying on CBO and Congressio-nal Research Service data), military compensation and health benefits (Defense Business Board and CBO), and acquisition (U.S. Government Accountability Office). As can be seen from Figure C-5, which the CSIS study team presented to the DDWG at its 25 September 2012 meeting, the conclusion drawn from its earlier work was confirmed—namely, that the combined effect of the defense drawdown and internal cost inflation would "crowd out" spending for modernization. In fact, the picture was even worse—in July 2012, we calcu-lated that that point would be reached in 2023, but our subsequent analysis indicated that it would occur in FY 2020.[23]

---

22. The second tranche of BCA caps were adjusted in January 2014 by the Bipartisan Budget Act, which reduced the "sequester cuts" for FY 2014 by $22.5 billion and for FY 2015 by $9 billion.

23. Our confidence in our "double whammy" analysis was strengthened further through an unexpected source, the analytic team of one of the defense "primes." Attracted by our May 2012 interim report, they briefed their analysis of DoD's defense budget in June 2012 and subsequently carried out a parallel investigation (using their own databases) of the DDWG methodology. We were pleased to learn in early September 2012 that their analysis replicated our results.

Table C-2. Cost Growth Assumptions

Cost Category	Illustrative Line Items	Appropriation Account	Annual Cost Growth above Inflation (per person)
Pay and retirement	- Basic pay - Housing allowance - Retirement	MILPERS	1.7%
Health care	- Defense Health Program Accrual - Medicare-Eligible Retiree Healthcare Fund Contribution - Military Defense Health Program (DHP)	MILPERS O&M	3.4%
O&M (excluding DHP)	- Maintenance and depot repair - Fuel and lubricants - Education and training - Logistics support - Operations support	O&M	2.5%
Military construction	- Major and minor construction - Family housing - BRAC	MILCON	0%
Acquisition programs	- Science and Technology - Major Defense Acquisition Programs	Procurement RDT&E	1.9%

Figure C-5. Internal Cost Inflation against the Projected Defense Topline

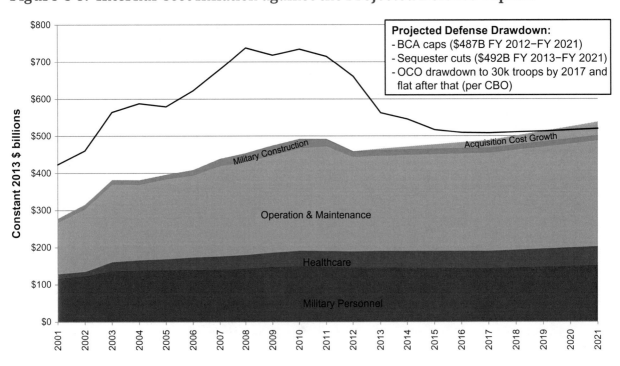

Figure C-6. The 2021 "Affordable Force"

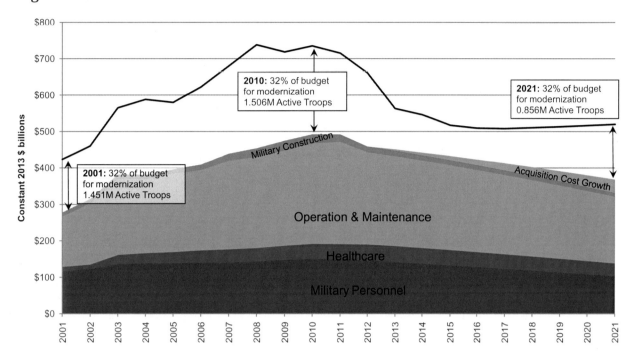

At the same time that it revalidated previous analysis, the CSIS study team also explored how much end strength DoD would have to trade in order to restore the normal share (about 32 percent) of the defense budget that was spent on modernization (RDT&E plus procurement). As will be discussed in more detail shortly, the CSIS study team held readiness (in terms of O&M per active-duty troop) constant and made reduced personnel the "bill payer" for modernization.

As displayed in Figure C-6, DoD would have to cut 661,000 in active-duty troops in order to free up enough defense dollars to restore modernization to 32 percent of the defense budget. After reviewing this analysis at the 25 September 2012 DDWG meeting, the CSIS study team released a short white paper on the "double whammy" effect of topline reductions and internal cost inflation on the defense budget.[24] The analysis in this paper has changed little and has been the basis of subsequent outreach and analytic efforts.

Figure C-6 also introduced for the first time the concept of the "Affordable Force." In his 12 September 2012 paper for the DDWG, Clark Murdock argued that a fundamentally different planning approach was necessary to cope with the severity of the "double whammy" effect:

> In the Affordable Force, we have identified how many people, how much readiness, and how much modernization DoD will get. These are the inputs that DoD uses when it "buys" capabilities. Rather than ask "how much is enough," we have asked

---

24. Clark A. Murdock, Kelley Sayler, and Ryan A. Crotty, *The Defense Budget's Double Whammy: Drawing Down While Hollowing Out from Within* (Washington, D.C.: Center for Strategic and International Studies, October 2012), https://csis.org/publication/defense-budgets-double-whammy-drawing-down-while-hollowing -out-within.

"how much can be spent." Only after we have determined how much can we spend, much like any prudent and frugally minded household, can we turn to strategy.[25]

Noting that almost all of the debate about the magnitude of the defense drawdown had focused on the defense budget topline, Murdock argued that the aggregate impact of these streams (personnel, benefits, O&M, and acquisition) of inflationary costs not only outweighed the effect of the topline reductions but demanded a new "cost-capped" approach to both controlling costs and suppressing ambitious strategic ends.

Origins of the Cost-Capped Approach

Despite decades of attempted defense reforms aimed at "changing the way DoD does business," the Department has been unable to control internal cost growth (see Figure C-1). Whether it was the Defense Reform Initiative (DRI) followed by the Revolution in Business Affairs during the Clinton administration or Defense Business Transformation under Secretary of Defense Donald Rumsfeld, the results were the same. In fact, DoD's track record at actually realizing cost savings from defense efficiencies is so poor that the CBO started in 2011 to provide, in addition to DoD's Future Years Defense Program (FYDP) projection, its own significantly higher "CBO projection" with the laconic footnote: "The CBO projection incorporates costs that are consistent with the Department of Defense's (DoD's) recent experience."[26] Although a longtime advocate of defense reform, Murdock finally gave up on the cause in a strongly worded statement to the DDWG:

> Despite the repeated efforts to change the way DoD does business, DoD has failed to manage its costs for the last two decades and is likely to keep on doing so. In a recent (8/15/12) Fortune interview, Republican Presidential candidate Mitt Romney said that he believes "we will find enormous opportunities for efficiency and cost savings in the military" and that he would use those savings to buy back 100,000 of the military personnel being cut to meet the BCA caps. The information above [see Table C-1 and Figure C-5] suggest that these kinds of statements are counterfactual in nature and that any defense planning predicated on the "negative funding wedges" made possible by as yet-to-be-achieved efficiencies is an exercise in self-delusion.[27]

Secretary Robert Gates began the defense drawdown when he announced in January 2011 that the planned growth in FY 2012 would be cut by 2.6 percent (or $78 billion). At that time, he also announced that the services had identified $100 billion in overhead savings that they would be allowed to reinvest in priority war-fighting and modernization programs and that DoD had identified $54 billion in savings through efficiencies and freezes in civilian pay and positions. Although there was considerable speculation that DoD was

---

25. Clark Murdock, *A Proposed Methodology for Preparing for a Deep Defense Drawdown* (Washington, D.C.: Center for Strategic and International Studies, September 12, 2012), https://csis.org/publication/proposed -methodology-preparing-deep-defense-drawdown.

26. Congressional Budget Office, *Long-Term Implications of the 2011 Future Years Defense Program*, February 2011.

27. Murdock, *A Proposed Methodology*, 5.

falling short in its effort to realize the Gates-projected $230 billion in savings, Secretary Leon Panetta in January 2012 tacked on another $60 billion in claimed efficiency savings during FY 2013–FY 2017. Stacking yet another unachievable goal on top of a stack of unrealized goals is not realistic planning; it is denial.

At the 25 September 2012 DDWG meeting, the CSIS study team proposed a "cost-capped approach" that was predicated on the following assumptions, which reflect existing political and policy realities:

- *The defense budget drawdown will continue on the path mandated by the Budget Control Act of 2011 and its sequester mechanism will be triggered on 2 January 2013.*
  - *No matter who wins the Presidential election, the political gridlock over tax increases and entitlement cuts will continue until it doesn't. To plan otherwise is foolhardy and contrary to how DoD does operational planning. In this instance, the "what if" question is "what if there is no sequester."*

- The deals reached in January 2013 (the American Taxpayer Relief Act) and January 2014 (the Bipartisan Budget Act) provided very limited relief from the BCA sequester caps: the first act reduced the sequester cut in FY 2013 from $55 billion to $43 billion (of which all but $2 billion applied to DoD) and reduced the FY 2014 sequester cut by $4 billion; the second agreement, as stated above, reduced the "sequester cut" in FY 2014 by another $22.5 billion and the FY 2015 cap by $9 billion. The two tranches of BCA cuts—$487 billion imposed in FY 2012–FY 2021 and $430 billion (down from $492 billion originally mandated by the BCA)—still comprise almost a trillion dollars in defense budget topline reductions. Despite recent events (such as ongoing strife in Syria and the Cold War–like standoff over Ukraine), there seems little prospect of significant relief from the BCA "sequester cuts."

- *There are no further politically feasible gains to be had from increased efficiency or, more broadly, "changing the way DoD does business."*
  - *In light of two decades of the persistent failure to control internal cost growth, assuming that DoD (and Congress) can change its stripes is faith-based, not fact-based planning.*
    - *NOTE: Those who argue that real reforms can generate real savings are correct, but those reforms are of the roles and missions variety, which involve major organizational and cultural changes, not business efficiencies. The Pentagon does not need to have at least six acquisition systems (Army, Navy, Marines, Air Force, SOCOM, and MDA) and eight requirement-generation processes (the previous list plus OSD and the Joint Staff). One of the consequences of this cost-capped approach is that it will make explicitly clear that the opportunity costs of failing to make real reforms in "how DoD does business" is the loss of strategic opportunities because the United States can't afford the capabilities necessary to take advantage of them.*

- *The cost-capped approach attempts to close the gap between ends and means by suppressing the appetite for expansive objectives (which many Americans seem to share) by limiting DoD's strategic options to the resources available to them—that is, keeping them inside the Affordable Force box.*

- *Putting resource constraints first as hard caps on our strategic choices should help curb the all-too-American inclination to attempt to solve all problems. This is about formulating a sustainable strategy, one that is economically and politically affordable. Those who want a more activist foreign policy or a bigger U.S. global role should bear the burden of coming up with the resources to pay for it.*[28]

The logic of using cost caps is well known to defense appropriators. Frustrated by increasing costs per unit (for example, the F-22), Congress "caps" the overall program at a fixed figure and, in effect, "tells" DoD that it can have as many units as fit under the cap. This is also the logic of the BCA—they are called "BCA caps" for a reason. And this is the approach we recommend to a secretary of defense determined to control costs. Instead of pursuing literally hundreds of separate efficiency initiatives, the secretary "caps" the total dollars for a particular function or activity and lets the implementers figure out how to make ends meet. If determined to achieve greater savings—as Congress was with the second tranche of BCA "sequester cuts"—the secretary can reduce the caps. While it requires discipline and intestinal fortitude, the cost-capped approach is easier, both bureaucratically and politically, than following up on all the individual promises "to change how DoD does business."

Reconceptualizing the Defense Budget

Although the CSIS study team continued to tweak the methodology—the May 2012 seven-step process evolved into a three-part (Supply-Demand-Balancing Supply and Demand) process with 11 separate steps—they increasingly focused on the macro supply-demand relationship between the defense budget, as capped by the Affordable Force constraints, and the key "must-have" capabilities needed to cope with the demands of the 2021+ security environment (see next section). As explained in a companion piece to the "double whammy" paper[29] and portrayed in Figure C-7, the 2021 Affordable Force Baseline[30] establishes a ceiling for how much military capacity can be "bought" in 2021 with fewer and weaker (in terms of purchasing power) defense dollars.

In a 12 November 2012 handout to the DDWG, the CSIS study team broke down the defense budget into two parts, the Institutional Force and the Operational Force:

- *Institutional Force: "the support infrastructure (e.g., training and recruiting, administration, etc.) that any future military will need to produce capabilities."*

---

28. Ibid., 6–7.

29. Clark Murdock, *Preparing for a Deep Defense Drawdown: The Defense Drawdown Working Group (DDWG) and the "Cost-Capped" Methodology* (Washington, D.C.: Center for Strategic and International Studies, October 2012), http://csis.org/publication/preparing-deep-defense-drawdown-defense-drawdown-working-group-ddwg-and-cost-capped-meth.

30. This was subsequently renamed the "2021 Sequester Force," because we applied, in the same manner that the BCA did, the cuts to the 2013 force structure in an across-the-board, "salami-slice" manner.

Figure C-7. Building the Affordable Force

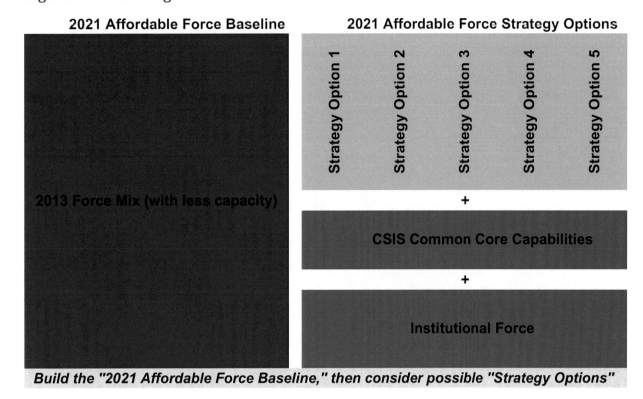

Build the "2021 Affordable Force Baseline," then consider possible "Strategy Options"

- Although the study team estimated, based on a detailed assessment of the FY 2012 budget, that this might comprise 32 percent of the defense budget, it also noted that a "should budget" approach, which copies the "should cost" approach to acquisition, could set the target lower, perhaps at 29 or 30 percent.

- *Operational Force: "Portion of the force that is employed in the conduct of military operations. Includes both those forces assigned to the Combatant Commands and those forces that are used in direct support of troops engaged in military operations."*

The maturing DDWG methodology further broke down the Operational Force into two subcategories, Common Core Capabilities and Strategy Options:

- *Common Core Capabilities (CCCs): "Those capabilities affordable at 35 percent of the budget to best address the most pressing (in the judgment of the study team) challenges in the 2021 environment."*
  - Note: While the basic concept that there would be a common set of capabilities that any 2021 military should have (e.g., global counterterrorism) received broad support in both the DDWG and AMWG, the term for these common set of must-have capabilities changed (from CCCs to minimum essential capabilities), as did the amount of the defense budget (from 35 percent to 63 percent) dedicated to them.

- *Strategy Options tradespace:* "Optional baskets of capabilities and capacity that policymakers may add to the foundational capabilities and capacity established in the CCC (see above). Policymakers would use this tradespace to increase the Armed Forces' ability to conduct missions in areas they deem most important beyond that provided in the CCC."

  - Note: The basic concept of strategic options tradespace was also accepted by both working groups, although the portion of the defense budget that should be used for this purpose varied from 35 percent to five percent. In drafting this report, we started with five percent of the defense budget, which amounts to $26 billion in FY 2013 dollars ($16 billion for force structure and $10 billion in modernization). As we tried to operationalize the five-percent-of-the-defense-budget approach across the strategic options, it became too unwieldy. We ended up by developing cost caps (at $228.5 billion in 2013 dollars for force structure and $1.8 trillion in 2013 dollars for FY 2012–FY 2021 modernization) for the 2021 Sequester Force, the 2021 Baseline Force, and the three strategic alternatives: Asia-Pacific Rebalance, Great Power Conflict, and Global Political-Economic-Competition.

Our use of the concept "institutional support" is not new. The U.S. Army, for example, uses the term "Generating Force" or, less commonly, the "Institutional Army" for what we call "Institutional Support." The same is true for the concept of the Operational Force, which is often used in discussions about the "tooth-to-tail" ratios in DoD. What was controversial was deciding how much did DoD actually spend on Institutional Support and the Operational Force (the "did cost" issue) and how much should it spend (the "should cost" issue).

Toward a Demand-Driven Statement of the Capabilities Needed for 2020+

Throughout 2012, Kelley Sayler revised with the DDWG several versions of a paper that characterized the 2020+ security environment as the demand function to which the DoD, as the supplier of military capabilities, responded. At the 25 September 2012 DDWG, the CSIS study team tabled a substantial paper[31] that "'Paint[ed] a Picture' of the Multi-Dimensional Demand for Military Capabilities" (Step D-1 of the DDWG methodology) and "Identif[ied] Potential Defense Implications of the Future Security Environment" (Step D-2). In its 18 December 2012 briefing at the final meeting of the DDWG, the CSIS study team emphasized the importance of balancing supply and demand:

- *Step S/D-1: Convert Demand for Military Capabilities into Metrics Used on the Supply Side*

- *Step S/D-2: Identify a Common Core of Capabilities That Each 2021 Force Alternative Will Have to Address 2021 Security Challenges*

- *Step S/D-3: Develop a Roster of 2021 Affordable Force Strategy Options*

---

31. Kelley Sayler, "The 2020+ Security Environment: Describing the Demand Function for the 2021 Affordable Force," Center for Strategic and International Studies, September 2012, http://csis.org/files/publication/121210_painting_picture.pdf.

Once the 2021 Affordable Force had been defined and quantified (which took six steps) and the 2021 demand for military capabilities (which comprised Steps D-1 and D-2 described above), balancing supply and demand involved first identifying those "must-have" capabilities (defined as force structure and procurement programs) that any 2021 military needed. In a sense, these comprised DoD's "mandatory spending" requirements in 2021. DoD's "discretionary spending" consisted of "nice-to-have" capabilities (again defined as force structure and procurement programs) that provided the basis for different strategic options. Under the cost-capped approach, it is this "discretionary account" that offers strategic choices to the policymaker. By contrast, DoD's "mandatory spending" is driven by the nature of the 2020+ security environment, particularly with respect to its "threats" (such as rogue states with nuclear weapons and violent Islamic extremists), and the changing nature of warfare (such as the growing importance of the cyber domain).[32]

At the 18 December 2012 DDWG, the CSIS study team presented the latest version of its evolving *Illustrative Primary Missions and Key Enablers* for the Common Core Capabilities (CCCs):

Primary Missions:

- *Counterterrorism (black and white SOF)*

- *Homeland Defense (steady state and surge)*

- *Project Power (how much is a critical issue) in an A2/AD environment*

- *Safe, secure, reliable and effective nuclear deterrent*

Key Enablers:

- *Intelligence, Surveillance, and Reconnaissance (ISR)*

- *Command, Control, and Communications (C3)*

- *Strategic Mobility*

While this slide provoked a lot of debate in the DDWG, it was more about capacity (how much capability is affordable) than capability (what kinds of capabilities belong to the CCCs). At the time, we portrayed the CCCs as accounting for 35 percent of the budget (approximately $170 billion in FY 2013 dollars); several DDWG members argued that this level of CCC spending was not sufficient to fully fund the four "primary missions" and three "key enablers."[33] Of particular interest was how much capacity for power projection was envi-

---

32. Subsequently during the Affordable Military phase of this study, a third component—maintaining critical American competencies (such as brilliant ISR or global precision strike)—was added to threats and the nature of warfare as the drivers of DoD's mandatory spending.

33. Over time, this view has prevailed. Although the term "Common Core Capabilities" was dropped in late 2013 and ultimately replaced by the "2021 Baseline Force" (which is the 2021 Sequester Force adjusted to reflect 2020+ threats, the evolution of warfare and the preservation of critical American competencies), the amount of the defense budget dedicated to this "mandatory spending" is 63 percent.

sioned: Was it enough to deter and defeat aggression? Was it sufficient to cope with two nearly simultaneous major combat operations (formerly known as major theater wars)? These are both long-standing defense goals that have greatly influenced DoD force planning constructs since the end of the Cold War. The response of the CSIS study team was that we do not know whether it is enough capacity; we do know that it is all that is affordable.

At this point, the CSIS study team had not spent much effort on developing a roster of strategic alternatives. At the 18 December 2012 DDWG meeting, they were presented with an illustrative roster of *"2021 Affordable Force Alternatives,"* each with 35 percent of the defense budget for discretionary spending on a particular option:

- *CCC Double-Down: spend all discretionary dollars on CCCs*

- *Assured Access (CSBA's Andrew Krepinevich)*[34]

- *Strategic Agility (Stimson Center's Barry Blechman and Russ Rumbaugh)*[35]

- *Kinetic Strike (CSIS): Emphasis on "hard power"*

- *Global Political-Economic-Military Competition (CSIS): Emphasis on "soft power"*

- *Others TBD*

As mentioned earlier, reserving 35 percent of the defense budget for discretionary spending was judged to be way too high. As will be discussed in more detail below, the force structure cuts needed to create this much "room" for strategic options were simply too draconian. The level of discretionary spending assumed in this report—five percent of the budget (about $26 billion in FY 2013 dollars)—may turn out to be too low, but that is the operative assumption at this time.

A Pause While Preparing for the Affordable Military Phase of the Study Effort

The paradigm for the year-long effort involving the DDWG was "preparing for a defense drawdown." As chronicled above, the maturation of the DDWG methodology, as well as the "double whammy" narrative that supported it, required near-constant revision within the CSIS study team and between the CSIS study team and the DDWG. Recognizing that further work of this intensity required external funding, Clark Murdock drafted a research proposal entitled "Building an Affordable U.S. Military: Critical Capabilities, Cost Caps and Clear Priorities." In the proposal, Murdock said that the proposed study:

---

34. Andrew F. Krepinevich Jr., "Strategy in a Time of Austerity," *Foreign Affairs* 91, no. 6 (November/December 2012), http://www.foreignaffairs.com/articles/138362/andrew-f-krepinevich-jr/strategy-in-a-time-of-austerity.

35. Barry Blechman and Russell Rumbaugh, *Strategic Agility Assessment of President's FY2015 Defense Budget* (Washington, D.C.: Stimson Center, March 2014), http://www.stimson.org/images/uploads/research-pdfs/Strategic_Agility_PB_Assessment_0318.pdf.

would be based on the premise that national security ends must be commensurate with DoD means. This "cost capped" approach would represent a new method of enforcing hard limits on the level of resources that can be allocated to a single purpose, seeking to constrain objectives to the resources available. In contrast to past studies, this approach would provide a means of fully accounting for the resource constraints on the Department, identifying necessary tradeoffs between end strength and modernization, considering reductions to existing force structure, and realistically counting efficiency savings.

While "preparing for a deep defense drawdown" was replaced by "building an affordable military" as the bumper sticker, the analytic foundation for both the successful grant proposal and the subsequent study effort was established during the 2012 DDWG study effort.

In addition to pursuing support for further analysis, Murdock continued to raise awareness of the double-edged economic vise on the defense budget. As mentioned previously, he gave a brief on "Defense Budgeting to Beat the 'Double Whammy'" at an 8 February 2013 session of the CSIS Military Strategy Forum, which was subsequently published as a CSIS white

---

Growing Awareness in DoD of the "Double Whammy" Pressure on the Defense Budget

In many respects, the biggest long-term fiscal challenge facing the department is not the flat or declining top-line budget; it is growing imbalance in where that money is being spent internally. Left unchecked, spiraling costs to sustain existing structures and institutions, provide benefits to personnel, and develop replacements for aging weapons platforms will eventually crowd out spending on procurement, operations and readiness—the budget categories that enable the military to be and stay prepared.

—Secretary of Defense Chuck Hagel, April 3, 2013,
National Defense University

[T]he [2014] QDR demonstrates our intent to rebalance the Department itself as part of our effort to control internal cost growth that is threatening to erode our combat power in this period of fiscal austerity.

—The 2014 Quadrennial Defense Review, Department of Defense

One of three "important initiatives" cited in the first paragraph [in the current fiscal climate is that] affordability is going to be key. It's easy for a political scientist to stand up here and say we need all these new capabilities and now all you engineers go out and build it, but we also need to add the requirement that we find ways to do this more affordably.

—Deputy Assistant Secretary of Defense for Force
Development David Ochmanek, March 18, 2014

paper.[36] As reflected in the accompanying text box, DoD was expressing growing recognition of the role of internal cost inflation in magnifying the impact of the defense drawdown.

Getting by with a Little Help from Our Friends

As discussed previously in the context of abandoning the July 2012 CSIS projected defense topline and adopting in September 2012 BCA-mandated budgetary ceilings, the CSIS study team recognized that the credibility of its analysis would be strengthened if it relied, to the extent possible, on analysis or data provided by authoritative sources. The first major instance when an external source "saved our bacon," so to speak, is in defining what portions of the DoD constituted Institutional Support and Operational Forces. Although convinced that the concept of Institutional Support made sense, the CSIS study team was struggling with how to operationalize it.

Initially, Ryan Crotty was exploring how the DoD breakdown of Major Force Programs (MFPs) could be used but was concerned that particular MFPs would contain both Operational Force and Institutional Force activities and that the data would not be granular enough. Then he discovered in October 2012 that the Defense Manpower Data Center had divided all DoD personnel between "Forces" and "Infrastructure." Somebody had already done part of the job for us: we now knew how much personnel was "institutional" and how much was "operational." Personnel breakouts provided a strong foundation for defining the remainder of the funding dollars into operational and institutional buckets. The initial cut can be seen in Table C-3 (and is discussed in more detail in Appendix D), and while small alterations were made along the way, the breakdown in Table C-3 provided the blueprint.

This did not answer the "did cost" and "should cost" questions. Crotty did a deep dive on the FY 2012 budget and calculated that Institutional Support comprised 32 percent of the budget. Shallower dives into the FY 2000 (pre-9/11 buildup) and FY 2010 (the peak of the 9/11 buildup) budgets indicated Institutional Support shares of 35 percent and 30 percent, respectively. This suggests that the Institutional Support portion of DoD's overhead is more fixed and changes more slowly than that portion of the overhead tied more directly to the Operational Forces (this issue is addressed more fully in Appendix D). The CSIS study team calculated that 32 percent was closest to what Institutional Support "did cost." At the end of DDWG phase, the CSIS study team took a "should cost" approach to Institutional Support and projected 30 percent of the budget as its targeted portion of the defense budget. This reflected the cost-capped approach that one could gain savings by putting a ceiling on institutional support costs. As its appreciation grew for the stubbornness of internal cost growth in DoD, the CSIS study team concluded that simply maintaining the level of Institutional Support at the 32 percent "did cost" level would be a heroic achievement for DoD managers and adopted 32 percent as its goal, especially as cutting institutional support

---

36. Clark A. Murdock and Ryan A. Crotty, *A Methodology for Making the Right Trade-offs in Defense for the Decade Ahead: Defense Budgeting to Beat the "Double Whammy"* (Washington, D.C.: Center for Strategic and International Studies, 2013), http://csis.org/files/publication/130417_Murdock_DefenseBudgetingDoubleWhammy_Web.pdf.

Table C-3. Defining the Operational Force and Institutional Support

Defining the Operational Force and Institutional Support			
Appropriation	Operational	Institutional	Methodology
Personnel	55%	45%	Used the division of personnel from the Defense Manpower Data Center, as split between "Forces" and "Infrastructure," then multiply by the cost per person in personnel account.
O&M	74%	26%	Divided O&M budget (O-1) based on Budget Activity: Operational Forces were considered anything in the "Operating Forces" and "Mobilization" activities, and Institutional Forces were the "Training and Recruiting", "Admin & Servicewide Activities", and "Environmental Restoration".
Procurement	75%	25%	Divided Procurement budget (P-1) by budget subactivity. Institutional: Support equipment and facilities, trainer aircraft, staff & infrastructure, base maintenance & support, chem and munition destruction. Everything else was considered Operational.
RDT&E	75%	25%	Institutional: all S&T budget activities - Basic Research, Applied Research, Advanced Technology Development - as well as "RDT&E Management Support". Operational included all other activities, which are ACD&P, SDD, and Operational Systems Development
Construction & Family Housing	0%	100%	All Construction and Family Housing activities were categorized as Institutional.
Total	68%	32%	

further than operating forces as a share of the budget would run against the trend of the more fixed institutional costs rising in share as operational forces draw down.

The second major assist came in March 2013 when CBO released its report entitled "Approaches for Scaling Back the Defense Department's Budget Plans." In this report, CBO more systematically provided its "CBO Cost Projections" as a comparison to DoD projections, which understated the projected extent of cost growth.[37] More important, from the CSIS study team's perspective, CBO had provided projected costs (both CBO and DoD) for military compensation and operations for 13 selected force structure units (Army BCTs, aircraft carriers, attack subs, Marine infantry regiments, etc.). This was truly "manna from heaven." The CSIS study team had known almost from the get-go that its methodological approach required a credible cost mechanism for future force structure units—after all, a "cost-capped" approach will work only if one knows the costs of the things being capped. This report initiated an extremely useful interaction between CBO and the CSIS study team that is discussed in Appendix D.

The Affordable Military Working Group (AMWG) Begins its Work

As can be seen from the list of participants at Appendix A, several members of the DDWG continued to participate in the AMWG, but several new members were added. This was

---

37. CBO amplified its previous footnote to its projections with the understated (but still laconic) notation: "CBO's cost projection of DoD's base budget is based on cost factors that reflect the government's actual experience and Congressional action in recent years." This latter reference, of course, reflected the fact that Congress had flatly rejected every DoD proposal to reduce the rate of growth in personnel and health care costs.

deliberate, as the CSIS study team wanted to maintain some continuity but also wanted fresh thinking. At the first AMWG meeting on 23 April 2013, the CSIS study team briefed "the DDWG methodology." While the overall approach remained the same, several important changes had been made since the last meeting of the DDWG in December 2012:

- The overly complicated three-part, eleven-step methodological approach had been quietly dropped.
  - The essential elements (e.g., "affordable force," Institutional Support and Operational Force, cost caps, etc.) of the DDWG methodological approach remained, as did the paradigm shift in defense planning: *"In this era of austerity, with severe pressures on the defense budget, the first question is not "how much is enough," but "how much is affordable?"*
- The amount of the defense budget dedicated to CCCs was no longer set at 35 percent of the budget but presented as a range that could change depending on feedback from the AMWG:
  - *[D]etermine how much capacity within the Common Core of Capabilities is affordable at 35 percent and 50 percent of the defense budget.*
    - Given these choices, decide how much capacity within the Common Core Capabilities is enough to address key 2021 challenges.
- Not surprisingly, given the maturity of the DDWG methodology, emphasis was given to implementation issues:
  - How Institutional Support was being defined and at what level of the budget.
  - Developing a methodology for "fully costing" force structure units:
    - The key chart (p. 50) of the CBO March 2013 report was distributed and discussed.
    - An update of progress on the demand side of the equation was provided, particularly with respect to the 2020+ security environment and the CCCs.

In subsequent meetings in 2013, the AMWG reviewed how the CSIS study team was implementing its methodological approach for how DoD should conduct a deep defense drawdown:

- 6 May: Reviewed how the CSIS study team divided the major budget activities (RDT&E, procurement, O&M, military personnel, etc.) between Operational Forces and Institutional Support.
  - When aggregated, Operational Forces comprised 70 percent ($455.5 billion), and Institutional Support comprised 30 percent ($193.2 billion) of the FY 2012 defense budget. The CSIS study team also presented a similar breakdown for the FY 2000 budget, which pegged Operational Forces at 65 percent and Institutional Support at 35 percent. This initiated the discussion that led the CSIS study team to finally set Institutional Support at 32 percent as both the "did cost" level (as the norm) and "should cost" target for the FY 2013–FY 2021 drawdown.

- 17 June: Reviewed CSIS study team's methodology for "fully costing" force structure notes.
  - As discussed in Appendix D, CSIS follows CBO's approach, but with one important difference:
    - CBO defines as overhead all DoD activities and costs *not* specifically attributed to forces directly involved in conducting military operations, as well as those forces supporting them. CBO then divides the overhead by the number of personnel involved, directly and indirectly, in operations and uses the overhead-per-person as the metric for assigning overhead to specific force units. Since Stryker BCTs have more personnel than Heavy BCTs (940 vs. 840), they have more overhead ($880 million vs. $730 million in 2013 dollars) attributed to them.
    - CSIS defines the total overhead in the same manner but then subtracts that portion of overhead that comprises Institutional Support (calculated at 32 percent in FY 2012 and targeted at 32 percent in FY 2021). The residual overhead is then attributed in the same manner that CBO does.
      - The primary reason CSIS factors out Institutional Support from all overhead is to implement its "cost-capped" approach for controlling internal cost growth. The CSIS team also believes that it makes sense to treat a portion of overhead as relatively fixed and not likely to vary much as total active-duty force structure increases and decreases. This conclusion was strengthened by its findings (reported to the AMWG at the 6 May 2013 meeting) that Institutional Support comprised 30 percent of the budget in FY 2010 and 35 percent of the budget in in FY 2000.
    - CSIS also follows CBO's practice of treating modernization (RDT&E & Procurement) cost for force structure units on a case-by-case basis, since each unit is at its own place on the equipment cycle (partially equipped, fully equipped, recapitalizing, etc.)
- 17 July: Discussed Vince Manzo's[38] paper entitled "Future Security Environment and the Common Core Capabilities." Although Murdock reviewed the remaining AMWG steps, the methodology itself did not change.
  - This paper was an updated version of Kelley Sayler's paper that was discussed at the 25 September 2012 DDWG meeting. The final version of this paper, which develops a demand-driven statement of the "must-have" capabilities needed in 2021 and beyond, is at Appendix E.

During the August–September break from AWMG meetings, the CSIS study team continued to refine its definition of the CCCs and, as chronicled in Appendix D, built its 2021 Cost Calculator.

---

38. Vince Manzo was a fellow of the Defense and National Security Group at the time of this publication. He has since left CSIS for employment in the Office of the Deputy Assistant Secretary of Defense for Nuclear and Missile Defense Policy.

Final Stages of the AMWG (Formerly DDWG) Methodological Approach and 2021 Cost Calculator

At the 2 October 2013 AMWG meeting, Ryan Crotty noted that each of the services had different approaches for defining which positions belonged to direct and indirect Operational Forces (both active and reserve) and to Institutional Support. For DoD as a whole and then for the services individually, Crotty reviewed how he proposed to proceed:

- DoD's Institutional Support would be divided into DoD-wide and service-specific accounts.

- All Operational Force costs are attributed to specific force structure units; Institutional Support costs are not.
  - Defense-wide operational costs are prorated across the services and then along with service-specific (both active and reserve) operational costs are attributed to force structure units.

- Using DoD's budget justification categories of Sub-Activity Groups (SAG), each service's Operational Forces budget was broken into direct (e.g., maneuver units and aviation assets for the Army), indirect (e.g., modular support brigades and echelons above brigade for the Army), and operational support (e.g., land forces depot maintenance, base operations support, etc.), each of which was composed of personnel and O&M costs.

Crotty concluded by presenting his initial tables of 2021 force structure unit costs (that is, in terms of the purchasing power of defense dollars weakened by FY 2013–FY 2021 internal cost growth) for each of the services. Although the feedback from the AMWG to the "Crotty Cost Calculator" was quite positive, it was suggested that we change the nomenclature for "Common Core Capabilities," in part because it sounded so similar to the "common core" terminology being used in educational reform.

Although the CSIS study team had planned to hold its final meetings of the AMWG in November and December 2013, the meetings were moved to 7 January and 14 February 2014 to allow further progress in using the 2021 Cost Calculator in applying the AMWG methodological approach and several significant modifications to both the methodology and the "double whammy" argument.

- As portrayed in Figure C-8, the CSIS study team used the 2021 Cost Calculator to provide a new "vivid particular" that demonstrated why DoD needed to adopt its recommended methodology. This visual conveys two powerful messages:
  - The 2012 military is simply not affordable in 2021, because it would cost approximately $237 billion more (in FY 2013 dollars) than the BCA caps will allow.

Figure C-8. Baseline Case: 2012 Force in FY 2021 Dollars

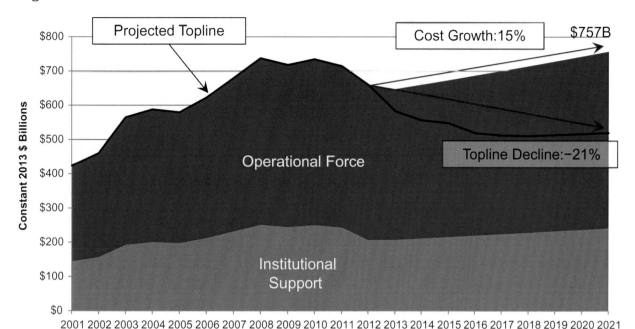

- Blame for this "dollar gap" is shared between the decreasing defense budget (which drops 21 percent in real terms) and internal cost growth (which increases 15 percent over FY 2012–FY 2021).

- The CSIS study team dropped the term "common core capabilities" and started using "minimum essential capabilities" but soon abandoned this formulation as well.

  - This term was derived from the 14 August 2013 paper by Vince Manzo, which stated: "Any future military, regardless of its broader national security strategy or alternative strategic priorities, will need some minimal capacity of the CCCs to cope with demands of the future security environment."

  - Although this formulation was used at the 7 January 2013 AMWG meeting, the CSIS study realized that this terminology implied that it was possible to define what level of capacity constituted that "minimum," when the reality was that one could define how much capacity was affordable at that cost point, not whether that amount of capacity was sufficient to cope with the identified threat (e.g., the global threat posed by violent Islamic extremists).

    - As will be discussed shortly, the CSIS study team stopped using this term as the methodology focused on adapting the "2021 Sequester Force" (that is, the 2012 force priced at BCA-capped FY 2021 dollars and defined by the across-the-board cuts mandated by the BCA) to 2020+ security realities.

- In response to AMWG feedback at the 2 October 2013 and 7 January 2014 meetings, the CSIS study team stopped assigning set values to the portion of the budget set aside for minimum essential capabilities (formerly known as Common Core Capabilities). During January 2014, the group settled on the following division of

Figure C-9. The 2021 Force

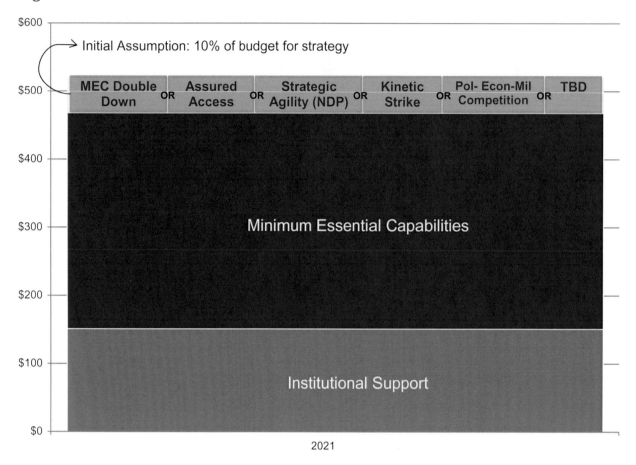

the FY 2021 Force redefined (according to the AWMG methodology), as shown in Figure C-9.

At the 7 January 2014 AMWG meeting, the CSIS study team presented the latest version of its "must-have capabilities" needed in 2020–2030:

- *Full-spectrum ISR, which is represented by "Global Force-Enabling Architecture" in the 2021 Cost Calculator*

- *Power projection against an A2/AD environment*
  - *The capacity of ground operations capability would be determined by the dollars available;*

- *Global direct-action CT capability*

- *Integrated theater and national missile defense*

- *Nuclear triad at levels sufficient to maintain parity with the Russia and superiority to China*

- *Military-technical superiority.*

Much of the session was devoted to discussing which components of these must-have capabilities should be increased (e.g., stealthy UAS, black SOF, etc.), which should be maintained (e.g., non-stealthy UAS, Marine force structure), and which should be cut (active Army, Navy carriers, etc.). The CSIS study team also discussed some of the problems they were encountering as they operationalized the modernization portfolio associated both with the 2021 Baseline Force and the Strategic Options.

As the CSIS study team used the 2021 Cost Calculator, it made several small adjustments to its sequential step-by-step methodology:

1. Cost the 2012 force structure at 2021 dollars that are capped at BCA levels.

2. Impose across-the board cuts to all force structure units until the overall force structure fits under the FY 2021 BCA cap.

   - This is called the "2021 Sequester Force." It could not actually be implemented because it consists of partial force structure units (e.g., 13.1 heavy BCTs, 8.8 carriers, 95.4 bombers, etc.). Moreover, as is argued in the report, across-the-board, salami-slice cuts is a mindless approach to force planning, which DoD, an adaptive organization, would never adopt.

3. Build the "2021 Baseline Force" by making adjustments to the 2021 Sequester Force to reflect the following:

   - 2020+ Security Environment, with an emphasis on threats.
     - When resources are scarce, coping with direct threats to Americans and their most important security interests takes top priority.
   - The changing nature of warfare.
     - Over the next decade, this means cyber and space; in the longer term, it could mean biological weapons.
   - Sustaining American key competencies.
     - Superior global situational awareness, a technologically superior force, etc.
   - Political and pragmatic adjustments.
     - The force structure (11 active and 3 Marine Corps reserve infantry regiments, etc.) are established in legislation and are unlikely to change.

4. "Make room for strategy" by cutting five percent of this force to create a tradespace for strategic options.

   - Initially, the team cut 10 percent (as portrayed in Figure C-9), but the loss of force structure to make this "bogey" was deemed too large and the target was ratcheted back to five percent.
     - This five percent tradespace totaled $26 billion (in FY 2013 dollars): $16 billion for force structure and $10 billion for modernization.
     - This ratio of 3:2 for force structure to modernization can be varied, although the percentage of procurement that goes to Major Defense Acquisition

Programs (MDAPs) is fixed at 35 percent, with the remainder going to "other" or "minor" procurement.

5. Build a set of options, with each reflecting different strategic assumptions and priorities, for spending $26 billion in FY 2021 dollars. The CSIS settled on the following set of options as it drafted this report:

- Option 1: Baseline
  - Restoring the five percent that was cut to "make room for strategy" is endorsing today's priorities (the FY 2012 force adjusted for FY 2021 fiscal realities). As stated in both the 2010 and 2014 QDR reports, the Obama administration's DoD sought to maintain forces flexible across the widest possible range of conflict. This option seeks to do that but with 21 percent fewer dollars, each with 15 percent less buying power.
- Option 2: Asia-Pacific Rebalance
  - Emphasis is given to both capabilities intended to counter China (in defeating its increasing A2/AD capabilities; holding targets at risk in mainland China, etc.) and additional presence in the Asia-Pacific to reassure China's neighbors.
- Option 3: Great Power Competition
  - Emphasis given to "hard power" capabilities for coercive diplomacy (including deterrence) of other major powers (China and Russia) and intimidation of and operations against "regional rogues."
    - Included diverting $10 billion from force structure and procurement to increase investment in RDT&E to force the pace of military innovation and maintain U.S. technological superiority.
- Option 4: Global Political-Economic-Military Competition
  - Emphasis given to "soft power" means (development assistance, Building Partnership Capacity, presence in Africa and Latin America, etc.) competing with other major powers at the peripheries of their global reach.
    - Included diverting $10 billion from DoD modernization to pay for nondefense means (largely financial assistance programs) to advance U.S. security goals.
- Choose one (or a hybrid option) and anoint it as the "2021 Affordable Military."
  - The recommended option in this report is Option 3.

At the final AMWG session on 11 February 2014, the CSIS study team updated members on the most recent changes in the AMWG methodology and reviewed a short, top-level "messaging" statement of that methodology. Murdock closed the session with very sincere thanks to all who had devoted their time to this study effort.

Final Adjustments to the Methodology as the Affordable Military Report was Drafted

As discussed in Appendix D, the 2021 Modernization Calculator summarized the costs of each MDAP for FY 2012–FY 2021, which (in its initial version) covered 82 programs, including investment placeholders for advanced systems (such as the new bomber) that would not be deployed until after 2021. This tool was applied as the 2021 Baseline Force was built from the base of the 2021 Sequester Force. The initial version of the calculator was too detailed and difficult to apply in developing the strategic options and was replaced by a calculator that included only the top 30 weapons programs. These 30 programs account for approximately 75 percent of the MDAP spending over the study period and include all programs that have a total cost over FY 2012–FY 2021 of $5 billion or more. The rest of the MDAPs were added to the 60 percent of the modernization budget that goes to "minor" or "other" procurement and treated as a constant variable that changed in proportion to the top 30 MDAPs.

As chronicled above, the issue of how much of the defense budget should be apportioned to the CCCs and how much for Strategic Options was much debated during 2013. The CSIS study team settled on five percent of the budget ($26 billion in 2013 dollars) as its operating assumption as it drafted the report. The process of adapting the 2021 Sequester Force to 2021+ strategic realities was straightforward—the judgments made were transparent and the resulting 2021 Baseline Force (both force structure and modernization) seemed appropriate. When Murdock cut that by five percent to "make room for strategy," the constraints imposed by the methodology seemed artificial. For example, the range on the number of carriers in the FY 2021 force was confined to eight or nine (the number in the 2021 Baseline Force) because $26 billion was enough to fund only one carrier. It seemed more appropriate to define different militaries (in terms of force structure and modernization profiles) for each strategy (that is, Baseline, Asia-Pacific Rebalance, Great Power Conflict, and Global Political-Economic-Military Competition) without limiting the variance between the options to any preset limit (like five percent of the budget).

The approach used was similar to that used by the CSIS analytic team (led by Murdock) in 2013 during the Center for Strategic and Budgetary Assessments–hosted "portfolio rebalancing" exercise. In summary, the first step was to build the 2021 Baseline Force, which was done by increasing (or "plussing up") the critical capabilities (beyond the 2021 Sequester Force levels) and cutting all the less essential capabilities in order to meet the Sequester Force Caps. The 2021 Baseline Force was used as the baseline (hence its name) for the other strategic options, again by increasing critical capabilities (e.g., additional carriers and Marines for the Asia-Pacific Rebalance) and then cutting less essential capabilities to meet the Sequester Force cap. The result was a set of strategic options, each with different force structures and modernization profiles, but all costing the same in 2013 dollars.

Figure C-10. Building the 2021 Affordable Military

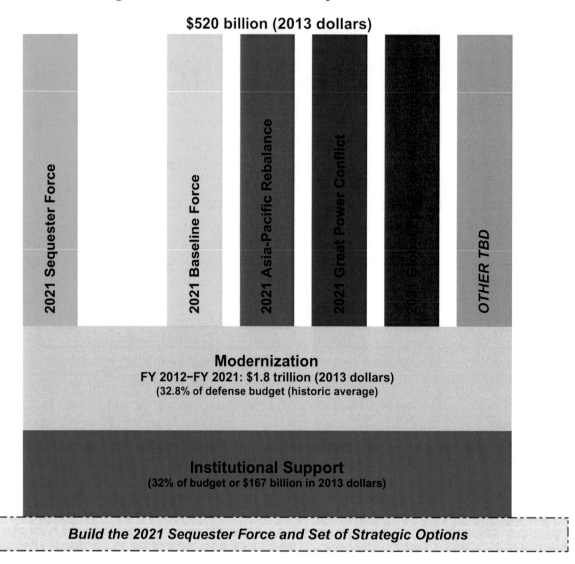

$520 billion (2013 dollars)

2021 Sequester Force

2021 Baseline Force

2021 Asia-Pacific Rebalance

2021 Great Power Conflict

2021 Global Role, From Mil. Competition

OTHER TBD

Modernization
FY 2012–FY 2021: $1.8 trillion (2013 dollars)
(32.8% of defense budget (historic average)

Institutional Support
(32% of budget or $167 billion in 2013 dollars)

Build the 2021 Sequester Force and Set of Strategic Options

Concluding Thought

The AMWG methodology evolved through a near-constant process of experimentation and adaptation, one that persisted through its final application in the drafting of the final report. Some elements of the methodology—the "cost-capped" approach, the 2021 Sequester Force, the 2021 Baseline Force, and so on—gained traction as they matured during implementation; others, such as the five-percent-to-make-room-for-strategy, evaporated in favor of something else (in this case, the "alternative militaries" approach). The intent—namely, to develop an approach for how the Defense Department should cope with a deep defense drawdown—has been firm. That said, the CSIS study team (with the help of its working groups in 2012 and 2013) has been flexible in its execution of this intent. How successful this process of intellectual discovery has been will, of course, depend on the credibility of the analysis in the report.

Appendix D: Costing the Future Force

Ryan A. Crotty

Introduction

One of the core objectives of the Affordable Military effort undertaken over the past year at CSIS has been, through both strategic and budgetary lenses, to demonstrate the trade-offs that are forced onto DoD by a declining budget and the weakening purchasing power of the defense dollar.

At the heart of that effort has been developing and executing a methodology to define and quantify the costs that make up the sum total of the Department of Defense in a way that those costs could then be manipulated in order to demonstrate those trade-offs. The key foundations of these trade-offs are (1) the magnitude of cuts required by the combination of topline cuts and internal cost growth, and (2) trade-offs within this squeezed budget environment demanded by a changing future security environment that forces the need to go beyond the inertia of across-the-board cuts to making strategically informed trade-offs between capabilities and capacity.

In order to facilitate these kinds of trade-offs, the CSIS study team developed an approach to breaking down the Department of Defense (DoD) budget that was targeted at ending up with usable chunks of force structure and modernization that could be employed to demonstrate the impact of the drawdown and inflationary pressures inside the defense budget, as well as the capabilities trade-offs that would be desirable for a correctly balanced future force.

The analytic tools developed for this approach were:

1) The 2021 Force Cost Calculator

2) The 2012–2021 Modernization Calculator

The foundational concepts underpinning the development of these two "calculators" were transparency and repeatability. It is in the service of these two goals that this appendix exists.[1] All data used were from open source materials. Although some data points do include information from conversations with people in government, no data used were from classified sources.

This appendix will first walk through quantifying the dual impact of a declining topline and growing internal costs above inflation. Then it will describe the CSIS study team efforts to reconceptualize the defense budget in order to implement mechanics for making trade-offs. Finally, it will address the building of the force structure and modernization calculators that underpinned the strategic trade-offs and targeted budget cuts seen in the main report.

Budget and Cost Constraints

The goal of the Affordable Military project was to demonstrate the combined impact of a declining defense budget and growing internal costs in DoD and use this aggregate impact to define the magnitude of the trade-offs necessary to accommodate the weakened defense dollar.

A SHRINKING TOPLINE

The first assumption that drove the budget scenario employed in the cost calculators was the topline decline in the overall defense budget. As discussed in Appendix C, the original intent of this project was to approximate the experiences of previous drawdowns and apply them to the defense drawdown today in order to understand the pitfalls of a drawdown and quantify the magnitude of the decisions and trade-offs facing DoD in the coming years. There was much debate early on about what the drawdown should look at (the magnitude, the glide slope, the connection to war funding, etc.). Possible topline declines considered included the average percent decline of the other three post–World War II drawdowns (37 percent), the average post-drawdown trough point ($383 billion, or a 47 percent cut), and a 33 percent cut to match the shallowest of the previous drawdowns. The group decided on an initial plan for a drawdown with an even annual glide slope and an end point one-third lower than the peak of the buildup, in 2024. Throughout this early process, the Budget Control Act of 2011 loomed in the background, but it seemed highly unlikely at the time that sequestration would occur and that these caps would be enacted. Nonetheless, by fall of 2012, it became increasingly clear that the BCA caps would indeed be enforced due to congressional stalemate over any grand bargain. Therefore, the CSIS study adopted the caps imposed after sequester as the baseline for topline reductions and revised the study period to line up with the enforcement period of the BCA, to FY 2021.

The BCA enacted two tranches of cuts to discretionary spending, each evenly split between nondefense and defense accounts. The first tranche cut the defense budget by $487 billion over ten years, from 2012 to 2021, by instituting budget caps on discretionary

---

1. The CSIS study team's decisions concerning trade-offs and strategic options are discussed in the main body of the report and in further detail in Appendix C.

spending. This cut amounted to a flattening of the expected growth in the defense budget. The second tranche applied another equivalent cut to planned spending, initially $492 billion by reducing spending caps by approximately $52 billion in each year from 2013 to 2021. Combined, the impact of these cuts would be almost $1 trillion over 10 years. While the second tranche, the so-called sequester cuts caused by the revision of the budget caps initiated by the failure to come to a deal over deficit reduction, have been revised twice and undergone one year of execution, they remain nearly $1 trillion over the 10-year period. Faced with a realistic glide slope and end point, the study team, in consultation with the working group, decided to adopt the cuts in law as the topline for the cuts taken in the exercise being constructed in the Affordable Military methodology. Figure D-1 shows the comparison of an illustrative one-third cut in the topline as originally discussed by the working group (blue line) with the cuts imposed by the first tranche of the BCA caps (dotted red line), and the revised BCA caps after the failure of the Super Committee and the execution of sequester (green line). The sequester-level caps represent the final topline used in the CSIS study.

The study team did struggle with how to handle war spending (referred to as Overseas Contingency Operations, or OCO, funding) and how it should be represented in the drawdown. A discussion of the impact of OCO on the costing in the study follows later in the appendix. But for the purposes of the topline, the CSIS study includes some OCO spending all the way out to 2021. The drawdown in OCO in this study's assumption is from CBO, with OCO declining from its peak of $175 billion in FY 2010 to a flat $25 billion, adjusted for inflation, out to 2021. Therefore, in 2021, the CSIS topline consists of a base budget of $498 billion down from its FY 2012 peak of $539 billion and OCO funding of $22 billion.

Figure D-1. Comparing Topline Reductions

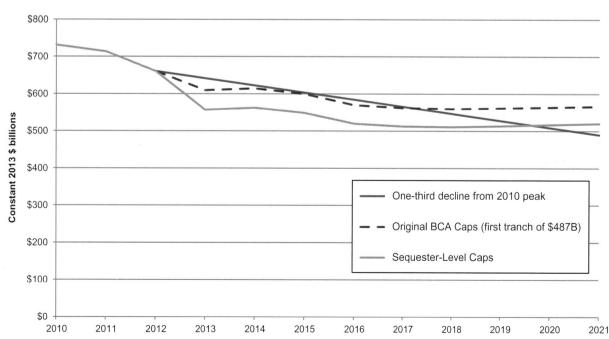

THE IMPACT OF INTERNAL COST GROWTH

Having defined the topline for the projected drawdown, the second step to setting up the infrastructure for making tradeoffs was to establish the baseline for internal cost growth. As discussed in Appendix C, the study encountered the evidence of internal cost growth in multiple sources and their own investigations of the changing cost structures of the defense budget over the previous two decades. It became clear that any projections looking out 10 years would need to account for the frequently unrecognized impacts of unbudgeted cost growth in health care, compensation, acquisition, and operations and maintenance (O&M). During the buildup and operations in Iraq and Afghanistan, the increase in these costs was overshadowed and enabled by the growth in the overall budget, subsumed in a budget that nearly doubled in real terms between the post–Cold War downturn and the height of the post-9/11 buildup. But as budgets began to creep down, recognition spread that while costs had skyrocketed over the past dozen years, the force had not substantially changed over that time period. The work of Todd Harrison of the Center for Strategic and Budgetary Assessments (CSBA) and that of CBO were particularly instrumental in informing the work of the study team recognizing the impact of this cost growth.

CBO has long tracked the growth of costs in DoD, tracking the differences between the FYDP submitted by the Pentagon and the expected costs based on cost modeling that recognizes that cost structures change over time. DoD has long based its long-term defense plans on an assumption that costs of things like O&M and pay and compensation will only grow with inflation or at the levels prescribed in the budget request. In reality, many of these costs are affected by outside factors, including the overall economy, programmatic issues, and congressional action. These differences can be absorbed by a growing budget with a large supplemental budget to accommodate war costs, but the impact is a buildup with little increase in troop strength but huge growth in costs, as was the case in the post-9/11 buildup. When the topline is declining, those unbudgeted costs cause significant problems in the year of execution. Therefore, the study team built a cost model that would include realistic costing to better demonstrate the impact of these increasing costs.

The internal cost growth model uses a number of different sources to establish a baseline of cost growth that could then be applied to the budget plan. These sources include CBO, the Congressional Research Service (CRS), and analysis of the historical trends in DoD's own documents. Different methods were investigated and tested for the various segments of the budget, and those that best approximated historical experience were used. In addition, representatives from one defense industry firm offered their time to run their own analysis without direction from CSIS (besides calibrating basic assumptions) as a check on the CSIS analysis. Upon comparison, the variance between the two models, using different methodologies was minimal. Figure D-2 shows the cost growth assumptions in each segment of the budget as utilized in the final analysis by the study team.

Figure D-2. Internal Cost Growth Model

Cost Category	Illustrative Line Items	Appropriation Account	Annual Cost Growth above Inflation (per person)
Pay and retirement	- Basic Pay - Housing allowance - Retirement	MILPERS	1.7%[1]
Health care	- Defense Health Program Accrual - Medicare-Eligible Retiree Healthcare Fund Contribution - Military Defense Health Program (DHP)	O&M	3.4%[2]
O&M (excluding health care)	- Maintenance and depot repair - Fuel and lubricants - Education and training - Logistics support - Operations support	O&M	2.5%[3]
Military construction	- Major and minor construction - Family housing - BRAC	MILCON	0.0%
Acquisition programs	- Science and Technology - Major Defense Acquisition Programs	Procurement RDT&E	1.9%[4]

1. Congressional Budget Office, *Long-Term Implications of the 2013 Future Years Defense Program* (July 2012), http://www.cbo.gov/sites/default/files/cbofiles/attachments/07-11-12-FYDP_forPosting_0.pdf.
2. Congressional Budget Office, *Costs of Military Pay and Benefits* (November 2012), http://www.cbo.gov/sites/default/files/cbofiles/attachments/11-14-12-MilitaryComp_0.pdf.
3. *Resourcing the National Defense Strategy: Implications of Long-Term Defense Budget Trends: Hearing before the House Committee on Armed Services, 111th Congress (2009), (testimony of Stephen Daggett,* Congressional Research Service), http://democrats.armedservices.house.gov/index.cfm/files/serve?File_id=c617fc4e-391c-4f79-b8c4-c47661d8440c.
4. Derived independently from historical trend analysis.
   Note: The cost growth assumptions are above inflation. Inflation assumptions are from CBO's annual Budget and Economic Outlook, which projects inflation at 1.9 percent to 2017 and 2.0 percent after that.[2]

THE 2021 FORCE AT 2012 PRICES

The combination of these two factors, a declining topline and internal cost growth, does not paint a pretty picture for DoD in the coming years. As discussed in the main body of this report, neither of these two aspects is likely to change in the near term. The pressure on discretionary spending in the federal budget is only likely to get worse as growing impacts of interest rates, debt service payments, and baby boomer demographic shifts all will add to the pressure of mandatory spending on the discretionary accounts, including defense. Internal cost growth has been on an upward trajectory since the advent of the all-volunteer force, and it has only accelerated in the past dozen years.

---

2. Congressional Budget Office, *The Budget and Economic Outlook: Fiscal Years 2013 to 2023* (February 2013), http://www.cbo.gov/publication/43907.

Figure D-3. 2012 Force and 2012 Prices

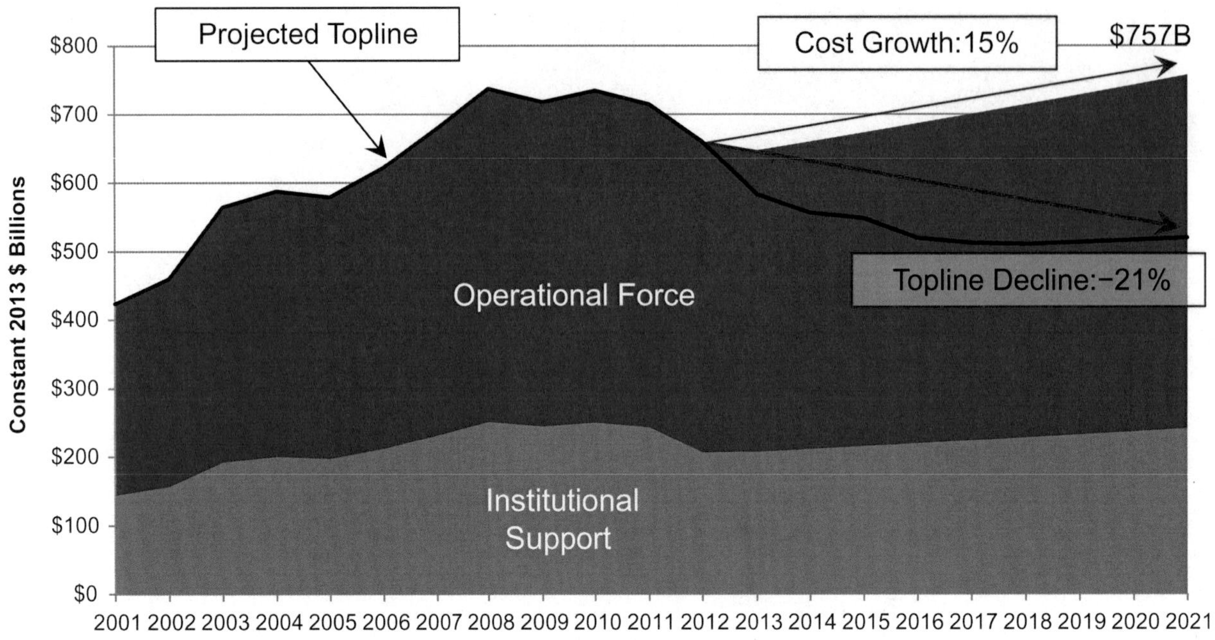

The combination of these two factors can be demonstrated by taking the 2012 force and looking at what it would cost in 2021. As shown in Figure D-3, in 2021, the force we had in 2012 would cost $757 billion dollars in 2021, a $100 billion increase in 10 years.

This is a 15 percent increase in costs over 10 years. But that is only the internal cost growth impact. Accounting for the decrease in total budget due to the BCA caps (the black line in the figure), there would be a $250 billion gap between the available budget and the cost of the force in 2021 alone. While this, of course, relies on an unlikely stasis in the force, including in OCO funding, readiness levels, and OPTEMPO, it illustrates the magnitude of the challenge at hand.

Creating the Building Blocks for Making Strategic Trade-offs

Having baselined projections of the defense budget topline and its fundamental cost structures, the next step was to break down the defense budget into its component parts. This would enable the rebuilding of the defense budget into the units of analysis required to make trade-offs that could illuminate the impact of cost pressure and provide a foundation for thinking strategically about capabilities and capacity in a budget-constrained context.

RECONCEPTUALIZING THE DEFENSE BUDGET

The budget of the Department of Defense is a massive and complex organism. It can be sliced up in many different ways in order to analyze the allocations of funding. A key step in this process was to reorganize the familiar ways of breaking down the defense budget in order to better enable the combining of the different pieces that go into force structure and modernization for turning into the building blocks described above.

First, it is important to be clear about the parameters of what is being moved around. So to begin with, a few assumptions: As a rule, all dollar figures referenced throughout this section are in Total Obligational Authority (TOA), which includes "all budget authority (BA) granted from the Congress in a given year, amounts authorized to be credited to a specific fund, BA transferred from another appropriation, and unobligated balances of BA from previous years which remain available for obligation."[3] In addition, all figures have been adjusted for inflation and are expressed in constant 2013 dollars. The baseline year for this study is 2012, the last year before sequestration, and the study period runs until 2021, the last year of the BCA caps (though later revisions extended parts of the cap mechanism out to 2023). All years cited are fiscal years.

Traditionally, the defense budget has been visualized in two different ways, by military department or by appropriation account—as depicted in Figure D-4. The Department of the Army, Department of the Navy (which includes the Marine Corps), and the Department of the Air Force, are typical levels of analysis for the budget, as they broadly represent different types of capabilities and are perceived to compete against each other for resources. There is a fourth segment broken out here, which is referred to as "Defense-Wide," which includes everything that does not reside inside the military departments, including the many defense agencies and activities that report to the Office of the Secretary Defense, the Joint Staff, which oversee the Combatant Commands, and the Defense Health Program. The sum of these four segments make up the entirety of the DoD budget. This can be seen in the top face of the cube in Figure D-4.

The second facet of the traditional method of segmentation is by appropriation or public law title, depicted on the side of the cube in Figure D-4. These segments match up with broad groupings of different types of government funds as they are appropriated by Congress. Actual appropriations occur at the appropriation account level (e.g., Aircraft Procurement, Air Force) but are usually rolled up to the title level for trend analysis.

- The *Military Personnel* account includes most of the direct costs of active and reserve personnel serving in the military, including basic pay, housing allowances, benefits, travel, and retirement. Often shortened to MilPers, this account typically comprises about one-quarter of the defense budget.

---

3. Office of the Under Secretary of Defense (Comptroller), *Department of Defense Financial Management Regulation 7000.14-R* (June 2011), http://comptroller.defense.gov/fmr.

Figure D-4. Traditional Segmentations of the Defense Budget

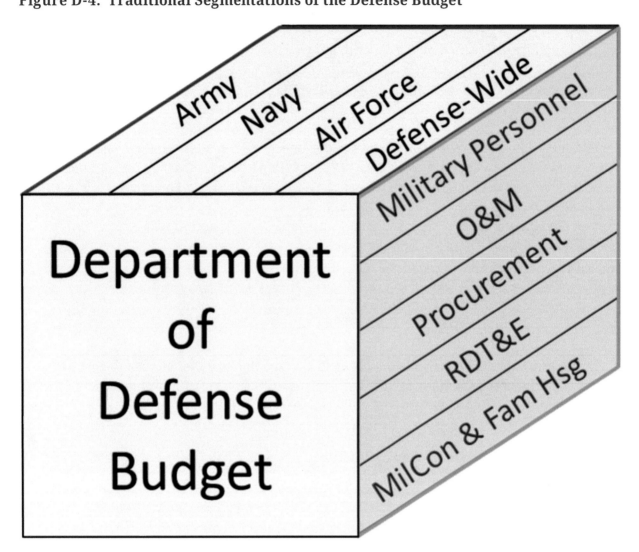

- The *Operation and Maintenance* (O&M) account is the largest of the appropriation titles, averaging 35 percent of the budget since the beginning of the all-volunteer force in 1973 and having grown to 40 percent of the budget in recent years. It thus covers the largest range of activities, including civilian salaries, equipment maintenance, fuel, supplies, base support, facilities maintenance, and almost all "operating expenses" of DoD.

- The *Procurement* account pays for investment in equipment above a certain threshold (as O&M buys many small and centrally managed items). This includes major weapons systems like fighter jets and ships, as well as munitions, service vehicles, information system, and major equipment upgrades.

- *Research, Development, Test, and Evaluation (RDT&E)* funds the full range of development of new technology for DoD, from basic research performed at universities or government installations to initial operational testing of new systems and equipment by contractors.

- Unlike the prior segments of the defense budget, *Military Construction* and *Family Housing* are funded out of a different appropriation bill along with Veterans Affairs (not included here) but still get included in the defense budget. Military Construction (MilCon) funds all construction above a certain threshold at military installations, and Family Housing funds improvements to the housing inventory through private-sector partnerships. For purposes of this project, these two appropriations are lumped together as simply MilCon.

The traditional segmentation of the defense budget described above is generally useful, but for the purposes of this study, an approach that both consolidates and separately breaks out these segments is preferred. To some degree, the traditional segments are preserved in the new breakouts, as DoD data are divided along the lines above. Nonetheless, this reconfiguration helps to manipulate the budget data in ways that are more attuned to the purpose of this study. Figure D-5 demonstrates the reconceptualization done by the CSIS team to better utilize the defense budget for analytic purposes.

Figure D-5. The Re-conceptualized Defense Budget

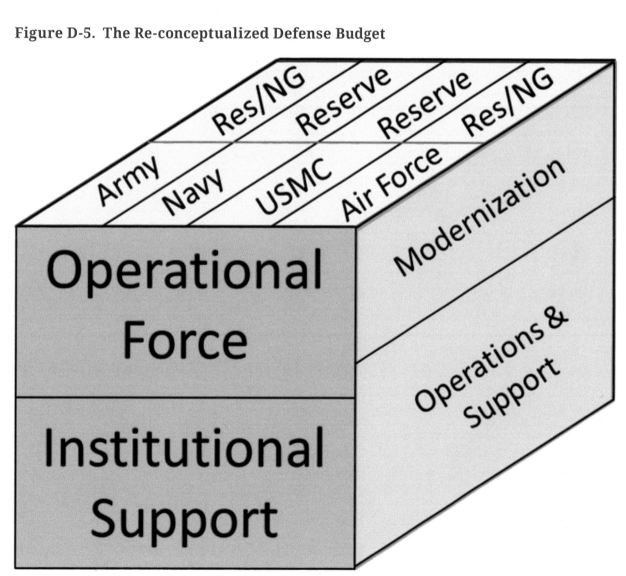

The military departments along the top face of the cube have been replaced with the military service components, which breaks each of the departments into the active and reserve service components, as well as breaking the Marine Corps out from the Navy. Furthermore, the Defense-Wide grouping has been eliminated. For the purposes of this study, Defense-Wide is treated as generally providing operational and institutional support to the services, without being an output of military force in its own right. Therefore, the costs associated with the Defense-Wide accounts have been distributed into the services as fully burdened costs, as will be discussed later. Whether it is the National Geospatial Intelligence Agency providing GEOINT for military operations or the Defense Contract Management Agency managing DoD's contracts and suppliers, these activities support the modernization and operations of the force and thus can be reconfigured to be rolled up into the service's costs. The outlier in the Defense-Wide accounts is Special Operations Command (SOCOM), which does indeed provide military capability. While all SOCOM military personnel are paid out of the service MilPers accounts, the operations and modernization for special operations units is paid for out of the Defense-Wide account. So, all SOCOM funding has been pulled out of the Defense-Wide budget and applied to each of the special operations unit costs within each service. In this analysis, the cost of each special operations unit is based solely on number of personnel in the unit; there is no other differentiation in cost between units.

The second reconceptualization, shown on the right-hand face, comes at the appropriation title level. The five appropriation titles discussed above have been rolled up into two large groupings: (1) operations and support and (2) modernization. Operation and Support (O&S) pays for all of the ongoing costs of operating and sustaining the force, costs residing in the MilPers and O&M accounts—including all military pay and benefits, maintenance, training, and civilian salaries. These costs will be turned into force structure units. Modernization sums all of the investment activities that DoD undertakes to support the future force. This includes all research and development efforts, procurement, and military construction. Modernization does not happen in a vacuum—old systems need to be replaced for force structure units to continue to be deployable, research needs to be done to initiate the next generation of technology and platforms, and bases need to be in shape to house DoD's people, forces, and support functions. Nonetheless, these costs operate outside of the day-to-day operation of the force in most cases. The treatment and assumptions of these two aggregated segments will be discussed in more detail later.

The final segmentation in the study team's reconceptualization of the defense budget, on the front face of the figure, divided all costs into "Operational Force" and "Institutional Support" costs. This division of costs differentiates between those that can be attributed to deployable force structure units and those that support the broader institutions that underpin the Department and the services. The breakdown between these two types of costs and its implementation will be discussed below.

OPERATIONAL FORCE AND INSTITUTIONAL SUPPORT

With the defense budget broken down to constituent parts, it was then time to rebuild into units that would provide the basis for making decisions about the size, shape, and composition of the 2021 force. The first step was to build a taxonomy that would enable the final output of the force structure and modernization calculators to focus on the fully costed elements of forces and platforms. Central to the effort to define and cost the force structure units in this analysis was to structure the costs in a way that separated out the costs that could be attributed to those force structure units—the costs that are required to support deployable forces and keep them running—from those costs that keep the Department and the military services running but do not directly support the sustaining and employing of military force. The CSIS team called these the "Operational Force" and "Institutional Support" and defined them thus:

- Operational Force: The portion of the force that is employed in the conduct of military operations. Includes both those forces assigned to the Combatant Commands and those forces that are used in direct support of troops engaged in military operations.

- Institutional Support: The support infrastructure (e.g., training and recruiting, administration) that any future military will need to produce capabilities.

This is the division that is most outside of the traditional discussion of the defense budget. Nonetheless, this is not an uncommon way for the services to think about their costs. This methodology essentially takes a broad view of the oft-discussed "tooth-to-tail ratio" across the whole force. Operational Force costs are those war-fighting tools available to the combatant commanders and the costs directly associated with manning, training, equipping, and maintaining those forces. Institutional Support costs are those foundational costs of the force necessary to maintain the integrity of the future force, which do not directly support combat forces but recruit, train, house, sustain, and administer the force. This takes an intentionally broad view of what makes the "tooth" in order to isolate those parts of the defense budget that will scale with the cutting and adding of specific force structure units and those that may scale with the size of the overall force but are stickier or fixed costs.

The study team proceeded to divide each of the budget appropriation accounts, line by line, into operational and institutional silos. The foundational documents for this effort were the budget justification materials provided by the Office of the Under Secretary of Defense (Comptroller). The actual division of these accounts is discussed in further detail later.

The original intent in making this division, as described in more detail in Appendix C, was the desire to use the proposed cost-capped approach to reduce infrastructure costs through the capping of Institutional Support costs across DoD. In light of further investigation of prior-year shares of Institutional Support costs, it appeared that, not surprisingly, in periods of budget growth due to combat actions, institutional support costs grow, but slower than that of the operational parts of the force. For example, in FY 2000, institutional support made up 35 percent of the budget, while at the peak of the buildup, FY 2010, those costs made up only 30 percent of the budget. While that margin may seem slim, during that peak year, five percent of the budget is over $35 billion. So, while the desire to limit Institutional Support costs was high, it seemed that the stretch goal for capping those costs might instead be to keep them from growing in share as the defense budget declined (i.e., to cut them at the same rate as cuts in the operational force). Therefore the study team fixed the Institutional Support costs for the study period at 32 percent of the budget – the same level as in the 2012 budget.

Separating out the Institutional Support costs was also critical for the other side of the equation—the force structure units. One of the goals of the costing of force structure was to move away from a narrow view of force structure (just the soldiers deployed in a Brigade Combat Team, the fuel to run the tanks, etc.) to a broader estimation that includes the additional costs of sustaining and supporting those "pointy-end-of-the-spear" units and making them deployable. By dividing the support costs between those that support deployable units and those that more broadly administer the Department and the services, this analysis draws a new line that seeks to better encompass the costs required for a force structure unit to function without additionally burdening those units with the far more tangential costs of having a functioning Department. This creates more fully costed force structure units, fostering the ability to trade off between force structure units in ways that include all of the associated costs.

The study team then took the definitions above and implemented them across each of the accounts, creating a functional division of every person and dollar in the Defense Department. These divisions are described below, by appropriation account title. There is no doubt that the distinctions below were often subjective in nature. There was spirited debate in working group sessions over the proper categorization of these line items, and no doubt some will disagree with these distinctions.

RDT&E: The RDT&E budget justification is divided into 10 budget activities. The study team decided that any RDT&E funding that could be directly attributed to activities in support of discreet modernization programs should be concerned operational activities while foundational science and technology (S&T) activities like basic research should be considered institutional activities. Therefore, budget activities defined as S&T by the Defense Acquisition University, 6.1 (basic research), 6.2 (applied research), and 6.3 (advanced technology development), are Institutional Support. In addition, 6.6 (RDT&E Management Support) is included in the Institutional Support activities, as it supports the testing infrastructure for RDT&E activities, including labs and ranges.

Once programs in the RDT&E spectrum have development and production plans within the FYDP, they are moved into the operational category, which is made up of 6.4 (Advanced Component Development and Prototypes), 6.5 (System Development and Demonstration), and 6.7 (Operational System Development). Definitions for each of the budget activities listed here can be found in the DAU ACQuipedia.

Procurement: Most programs that migrate from development into procurement phases would be categorized as Operational Force budget items. But the procurement account is made up of a lot more than simply big platforms and munitions. Procurement is also not organized as neatly as some of the other accounts. There are not discreet budget activities that carry through every service and subactivity. Each budget code simply describes another subset of procurement activities. Therefore, the study team scrubbed all thousand budget lines in the procurement justification materials to identify, to the degree possible, all line items that were for nontactical support equipment. This included everything from commercial vehicles to repair equipment to industrial facilities. Once these were weeded out, the rest was considered operational force procurement.

Operation and Maintenance: The O&M funding account is the largest, making up 40 percent of the total budget in 2012. Each service divides up its O&M funding differently. But the constant between all the services is the budget activity level. Every line item is divided into five budget activities. Budget activities (BA) 1 and 2, "Operating Forces" and "Mobilization," respectively, are categorized as operational. These activities include combat and combat support forces and service supports like readiness support and base operations. BA3 (Training and Recruitment), BA4 (Administration and Service-wide Activities), and BA10 (Environmental Restoration) are Institutional Support—including subactivities like central supply and logistics, transportation, basic training, and education.

Military Personnel: The budget activities for MilPers do not break along functional lines. The budget codes align with different compensation types, like basic pay, housing allowances, retirement accrual, and travel. This is completely disconnected from breaking down individuals by their job, station, or unit in ways that would facilitate an institutional or operational categorization. Therefore, the study team had to look elsewhere for classifications of military personnel. At first, the team sought to add up the numbers of individuals needed to man operational units (e.g., how many personnel are in a Brigade Combat Team). The challenge was to additionally account for all of the individuals in combat support—all of those in units assigned to higher echelons that are not attached to the force structure unit directly but are crucial to supporting the combat capability of those units (e.g., fire brigades). Even more difficult is establishing those in combat service support—those that make a unit deployable and service it but that may not, in fact, be directly providing combat capability themselves.[4] That effort stalled there. Fortunately, a classification system does exist in the public domain: the Defense Manpower Requirements Report. This annual report by the Defense Manpower Data Center divides up every billet in DoD into "Forces" and "Infrastructure." By using these "Forces & Infrastructure Codes" (F&IC), the team could isolate those military personnel in institutional roles and separate them from those belonging in operational force positions. Once this breakdown was determined, the military personnel budget for each service component could be divided by the number of military personnel in each function, providing a per-person budget breakdown to apply to Institutional Support and Operational Forces.

---

4. Ronald E. Porten, Daniel L. Cuda, and Arthur C. Yengling, *DoD Force & Infrastructure Categories: A FYDP-Based Conceptual Model of Department of Defense Programs and Resources* (Alexandria, Va.: Institute for Defense Analyses, 2002).

Figure D-6. Appropriation Account Breakdown of Operational Force and Institutional Support Funding

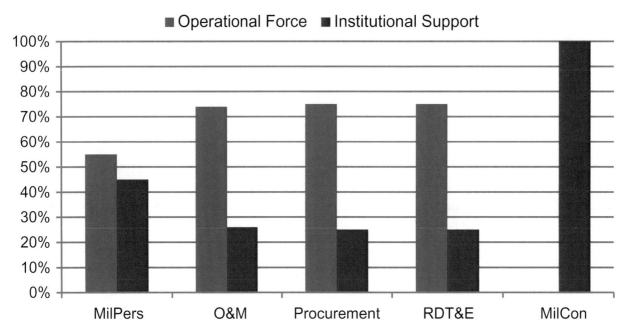

Military Construction: All military construction was deemed part of the institutional foundation of the force. Facilities, although in some ways enabling, do not provide or support combat capability in their own right.

Figure D-6 shows the breakdown as a percentage of total dollars in FY 2012 between institutional support and operational forces using the taxonomy above.

Because of the subjective nature of the breakouts described above, the study team undertook a quick sanity check by looking at the division of the Major Force Programs (MFPs) in the 2012 budget. An MFP is "an aggregation of program elements (PEs) that reflects a force or support mission of DoD and contains the resources necessary to achieve an objective or plan."[5] The 11 MFPs can be seen in Figure D-7. Program Elements are budget line items one level below what is available in the open source. Therefore, to those not in DoD, MFPs are too high a level of aggregation to be overly useful in a budget deep dive, but they are loosely divided into combat forces programs and non–combat forces programs. The percent division between operational and institutional segments of the budgets matched exactly to the CSIS analysis that tracked account by account. Although there is a degree of coincidence to this exact matching, as there is certainly different characterization of how the two segments are divided in the different methodologies, it was instructive and validating to have another source confirm the general breakdown between types of costs.

With the division of the operational forces and institutional support function accomplished, it is time to set aside the institutional segment and focus on turning the

---

5. Defense Acquisition University, *Glossary of Terms*, http://dap.dau.mil/glossary/Pages/2192.aspx.

Figure D-7. Major Force Programs, Combat and Noncombat

Combat Forces Programs			Noncombat Forces Programs		
MFP #	*Title*	*% of 2012 Budget*	*MFP #*	*Title*	*% of 2012 Budget*
1	Strategic Forces	2%	6	Research & Development	7%
2	General Purpose Forces	40%	7	Central Supply & Maintenance	5%
3	C3, Intel, & Space	14%	8	Training, Medical, & Other	14%
4	Mobility Forces	3%	9	Admin & Assoc. Activities	4%
5	Guard & Reserve Forces	7%	10	Support of Other Nations	2%
11	Special Ops Forces	2%	12	Other	0%
Total		**68%**	**Total**		**32%**

operational force segments of the various appropriation accounts from budget line items into aggregated, fully burdened force structure units and modernization profiles.

Developing the 2021 Force Cost Calculator

The next step in this process was to take the operational costs described above and ascribe them to force structure and modernization as outlined above. This section will deal with the division and attribution of costs to force structure units. First, it will describe the overall approach to developing a fully burdened cost structure; then it will identify the individual issues faced in each military service.

The study team decided early on that the primary level of analysis would be force structure. If trade-offs were going to be made, then the outputs of military force as demonstrated by the deployable units of the military services would have to be the focus of the budget analysis. The starting point for the list of force structure elements that the study team would seek to cost out came out of the 2010 Quadrennial Defense Review, which included a list of the "Main Elements of U.S. Force Structure." The study team used the 2010 QDR list as an aspirational list of force structure elements to be costed out in the study. Over time this list morphed based on availability of data and the work done by others in this area. Figure D-8 shows the final elements costed in this study.

The original intention for the study was for these force structure elements to be inclusive of all funding required to man these units, as well as the operation and maintenance funding required to operate and sustain them and the modernization spending to equip them. It became clear during the course of the study that, while the goal of including modernization funding that was tied to force structure would be ideal, in many cases modernization decisions are not directly tied to force structure and that connecting these two pieces in the model overly complicated attempts to make comparable force trade-offs.

Figure D-8. Force Structure Elements

Army
Heavy Brigade Combat Teams
Infantry Brigade Combat Teams
Stryker Brigade Combat Teams
Army SOF Battalions
Combat Aviation Brigades

Navy
Aircraft Carriers (Excluding Aviation)
Surface Combatants
Amphibious Ships
Nuclear Attack Submarines (SSN)
Ballistic Missile Submarines (SSBN)
Missile Submarines (SSGN)
Naval Aviation
Naval Special Warfare Teams

Marine Corps
Infantry Regiments
Marine Air Groups
Special Operations Battalions

Air Force
Bombers
Fighters
Transport/Tankers
Aerial ISR
Special Operations Battalions
ICBMs
Global Force Enabling Architecture

In addition, trade-offs in defense are often structured as trade-offs between force structure and modernization, and by tying them together, this would preclude those kinds of decisions being possible. Therefore, modernization is treated separately in, and the team devised, two different calculators for making force structure and modernization decisions. So, with the end goal of being able to trade within and between force structure and modernization, the team set out to categorize and deconstruct the entirety of the defense budget and then turn it into these building blocks. These building blocks would then be incorporated into the two "calculators" that would enable the team to adjust both the size and shape of the force in 2021.

A key component of understanding how to build the force structure costing model was better understanding the associated costs. It was at this point that the study team became aware of a parallel effort being undertaken by CBO to develop approaches to budget cuts in DoD. The CBO report of March 2013 "Approaches to Scaling Back the Department of Defense's Budget Plans"[6] demonstrated a blueprint from the same kind of analysis being undertaken by the study team. The CSIS team closely studied the work done by CBO in their report, noting both the similarities in approach and the differences. Most notably, CBO used a more fully burdened approach to the force structure costs that include what CSIS

---

6. http://www.cbo.gov/sites/default/files/cbofiles/attachments/43997_Defense_Budget.pdf. See, in particular, pages 18–20.

Figure D-9. Building Force Structure Unit Costs

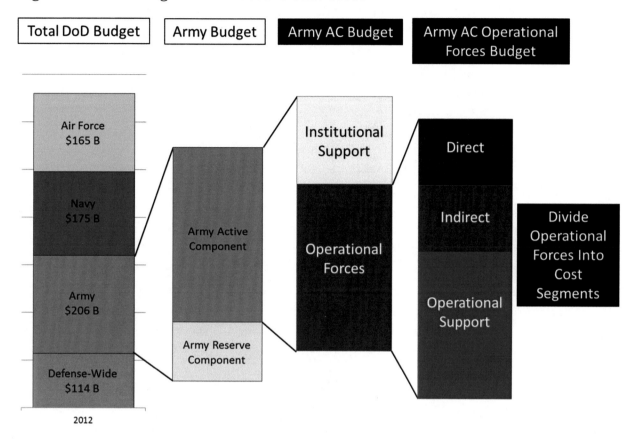

separates out as institutional support. So, while CBO categorized costs as direct, indirect, or overhead, CSIS included a distinction between operational support costs and institutional support costs, instead of lumping them together as overhead. After analyzing this comparison, the CSIS study team met with members of the CBO National Security Division to test the understanding of their methodology in comparison to the CSIS approach and ask for any constructive feedback on the CSIS methodology. Any flaws in the CSIS study team analysis are attributable to the CSIS authors alone.[7] Figure D-9 visualizes how all of these pieces in the CSIS approach fit together, using the example of the Army Active Component (AC).

Direct activities are the actual force structure units listed earlier in this appendix: brigade combat teams, destroyers, bombers, and so on. These are the outputs of military force, providing military capability for employment by the combatant commanders. Indirect activities are those combat support functions that do not reside inside the direct combat units but are key enablers within the services. For example, this is most apparent in the Army, where fires, battlefield surveillance, maneuver enhancement brigades, and many others are in separate line items from the direct units. This approach is slightly differentiated from CBO, which includes such things as transportation and maintenance in

---

7. CSIS would like to take this opportunity to recognize the great work done by CBO in setting the gold standard for this kind of analysis.

their indirect costs, whereas CSIS includes these items in operational support. CSIS then establishes a third category of operational costs, which are termed operational support costs—funding the activities that support the sustainment, readiness, and maintenance of the force structure units. CBO's third category, "Overhead," incorporates many items that CSIS separates out into institutional support as well as some operational support costs. The advantage of this approach is that it enables the policymaker to have more fidelity on the full cost of force structure units and to move them around as desired.

Every operational force dollar in the MilPers and O&M accounts, as defined by the division of operational and institutional costs described earlier in this appendix, is attributed to one of these three categories. A rundown of how this was implemented into each military service is described below. Each of the cost segments (direct, indirect, and operational support) is made up of two sets of costs: personnel costs and O&M costs. But, these costs do not divide evenly along the appropriation account lines. Personnel costs include all MilPers—which houses retirement, Medicare-Eligible Retirees Healthcare Fund, and almost all other benefits—but also include the health care costs that reside in O&M through the Defense Health Program, which has its own defense-wide appropriation. So, by taking the MilPers costs in each service, dividing it by the number of individuals in that service, then adding a per-person cost for the Defense Health Program, the team was able to establish a per-person cost in each service. One important assumption about personnel costs is that for the purposes of this study, each military person is assumed to cost the same amount within each service (as determined by the equation above). There is no differentiation between officers and enlisted personnel, nor between individuals with different jobs, pay scales, combat pays, and so on. There is differentiation between the costs of individuals between different components—Air Force reservists and Navy active-duty sailors do have different cost structures in this model based on the different costs inside of each component's budget.

The second input to costs of force structure is the O&M cost. This encompasses all of the costs required to operate, train, and sustain military forces. The inputs to this all come from the justification books for DoD and the services. Within each military component, there are three layers of specificity to the budget line items. The first is the Budget Activity, which was explored in the institutional/operational breakdown before to determine the division into those two categories. One layer below that is the Activity Group, which provides a smaller group of line items, and then below that is the individual line items called Sub-Activity Groups (SAGs). Below that would be the Program Elements (PEs) mentioned earlier, but these are not for public distribution. Therefore, the CSIS study team decided how to divide costs among the direct, indirect, and operational support categories based on the descriptions of the various SAGs in each service component's budget materials.

A significant aspect of O&M spending is civilian salaries and contractors. In this analysis, neither civilians nor contractors are varied separately from force structure, modernization, or institutional support. Both civilians and contractors would scale with the budget lines in which they are funded. For example, approximately 75 percent of civilians fall into institutional support, and thus the number of civilians would vary with the total institutional support topline. Contractors would vary with the O&M or modernization line items in which they are funded. Next, we will describe how the operational force and institutional support classifications were made for each service and how the related costs were then divided into force structure.

Another key assumption about the allocation of direct, indirect, and operational support costs is that, at a base budget level, these costs are fixed to the force structure unit. By using 2012 as the base year of this study, focusing on base budget costs (as described in the box below), the study team created an inherent bias that 2012 force costs are indicative of the costs to operate a unit in any given year. This assumes that the readiness and support funded for each unit will not change during the drawdown. It also means that this methodology does not account for force restructuring changes that may occur to rebalance the force inside of a service. In particular, this applies to the Army, which is undergoing changes in structure for both its aviation and land forces units. The units shown in the study are as they stood in 2012, without the additional battalion added to BCTs or the movement of Apaches and Blackhawks between the active and reserve combat aviation units proposed in the 2015 budget. So the level of 2012 readiness became the standard for the readiness assumptions in each subsequent year for this study. Similarly, the absolute costs for each force structure unit are also fixed at 2012 levels. This essentially means that the study accepts that, for example, the level of combat service support funded for a BCT in 2012 (in the base budget) is the "right" amount. Similarly, it assumes that the indirect supporting costs for a unit (e.g., maneuver enhancements brigades) were, in 2012, at the right ratio to the number of total units and that they will also fluctuate with the number of units in the force. Concern was raised at one presentation of this methodology that some indirect units do not scale evenly due to a constellation-like requirement and thus scale in a stepwise function. The example used at that time was that setting up a communications system in theater requires 100 percent of that unit—50 percent of a comms system provides zero utility. The team understands this reality, but the level of detail available in budget data does not enable this granular an approach.

COSTS BY MILITARY SERVICE

Below, we will describe the division of costs between each force structure unit within each service. There is a relatively high degree of specificity in how each cost was attributed to each force structure unit, but due to the limitations of open source budget data, these costs should be considered on an order of magnitude level.

Army

The Army in this analysis is divided into three types of force structure: land forces, aviation assets, and special operations battalions (SOF). The land forces are divided into the three types of Brigade Combat Teams: Heavy (or Armored), Infantry (Light), and Stryker. The direct costs for these forces come from the Maneuver Units line item, which explicitly states that it funds the modular force as defined by these force structure units. Direct

Explanatory Note on OCO Funding

The figures used in the costing are base budget costs. There was much debate among the study team over the use of base budget or base plus war funding (OCO). While costs in wartime naturally escalate because of the additional costs of combat pay, pay for reserve units on active duty, and operating and maintaining units overseas in a combat environment, there is also substantial evidence that many items being funded in OCO accounts will eventually (presumably over the course of the study period) need to be absorbed back into the base budget. Some items were simply moved into OCO for convenience and might be easier to separate out (the funding of F-22s, clearly not a war funding item); others are more complicated as costs that might be higher now, but parts of which will remain when these units are moved back to the United States and still need to pay for regular training, ammo, or other items that have been wholly moved into OCO. In the end, the study team chose not to overinflate the costs of steady-state, peacetime operations through inclusion of OCO funding, but note here that there will be additional pressures on the budget topline in the medium term due to the need to reabsorb some of these costs (which some estimate as at least $10–$20 billion) back into the base budget—to an even greater degree than expressed here.

Given this, the impact of the 21 percent topline decline and 15 percent growth in internal costs is not applied equally across each segment of the budget due to the variable impact of OCO on each account and thus cannot be aggregated directly to a 36 percent total impact on capability and capacity. The drawdown in OCO in this study's assumption is from CBO, with OCO declining from its peak of $175 billion in FY 2010 to a flat $25 billion, adjusted for inflation, out to 2021. The impact of excluding OCO varied across the different accounts, leading to a variable relationship between topline reduction, internal cost growth, and total necessary cut in any given set of costs. Those segments of the budget that experienced the most significant growth in costs from OCO will similarly experience the least squeeze during the drawdown. This is why the operational force structure cuts are approximately 15 percent, which is equivalent to the amount of internal cost growth experienced over the buildup. Costs affected by force structure cuts make up 46.5 percent of the budget (this is Operational Personnel + Operational O&M). In 2012, this was $306 billion. A 21 percent decrease from $306 billion would be $242 billion—which is indeed the amount of Personnel and O&M money in our 2021 force. This is an absolute cut of $65 billion. The big issue is that $81 billion of the $117 billion in total 2012 OCO is in Operational O&M and MilPers. OCO takes an 81 percent cut to go from $117 billion down to the amount we've been using in our glide slope—$21 billion. That 81 percent cut out of the $81 billion for Operational O&M/MilPers in OCO amounts to $66 billion in absolute cut—meaning only $1.5 billion needs to be cut out of Base Operational O&M/MilPers to reach the 21 percent topline cut in Operational O&M and Milpers.

personnel levels for each BCT type were determined by their relative sizes and the number of people funded in the Maneuver Units line item. The indirect costs are funded through the line items above the BCT level: the Modular Support Brigades, Echelons Above Brigade, Theater Level Assets, and Strategic Mobility SAGs. These include many indirect functions, such as brigades for battlefield surveillance, maneuver enhancement, fires, sustainment, signals, air defense, engineers, and medical services. The personnel attributed to indirect functions was determined by the number attributed to the four SAGs for indirect costs in the O&M books, divided out among the three BCT types using the ratio of direct soldiers attributed to those BCTs.

The combat aviation brigades (CABs) have their own line item: Aviation Assets. By definition in the description of the budget item, all direct and indirect costs for these force structure units are lumped together, including the CABs themselves, as well as echelons above brigade, theater level aviation, aviation support, and so on. Some have suggested that CABs should themselves be treated as indirect elements supporting the land forces, but it was decided in consultation with the working group that it made sense to make the CABs variable independent of the BCT force structure.

SOF in each service was broken out separately in order to vary them, consistent with each strategic option. Nonetheless, SOF does not get broken out separately in the budget documents and is treated differently in every service. Army Special Operations Brigades are aggregated together, even though there are different types that have variations in composition (Green Berets, Rangers, Civil Affairs, etc.) The special operations forces reside in the indirect cost line items in the Army budget along with the many other combat support units. The costs were derived by taking the number of Army personnel identified in the SOCOM budget justification books and applying costs based on the per-person O&M and personnel costs.

Finally, the remaining support functions for readiness, sustainment, facilities and base support, headquarters, COCOMs, and maintenance were divided among each force structure unit according to their share of direct and indirect personnel. Then the small operational portion of the defense-wide O&M (which is essentially for the Joint Chiefs of Staff and Classified Programs) also has a share spread across each Army force structure unit, as it does for every unit in each service in this model.

Navy

Navy force structure is centered directly on platforms. The ships of the fleet provide the primary capabilities of the service, and thus Navy platforms are equated to force structure units. There was discussion of making changes at the more aggregated level of Carrier Strike Groups and amphibious task groups, but this did not allow for enough flexibility and variability in decisions. In addition, these large aggregated units are frequently utilized outside of these traditional structures, and the composition of these groups changes. Therefore, surface combatants, carriers, amphibious ships, submarines, and aviation are used as the pieces of force structure to be traded in this effort. A few important notes on force structure: aircraft carriers and their carrier air wings are treated separately. This is first due to the separation of air operations and ship operations in the budget data but also because there is one more carrier air wing than there are carriers (in the active component). Carrier air wings are the primary combat unit of naval aviation and thus are the force structure unit being traded off. But included in naval aviation as indirect support are the other pieces of naval air that may not be considered directly in a carrier air wing, including lift/logistics aircraft, unmanned aerial vehicles, and land-based maritime patrol aircraft (P-3 and P-8A squadrons). For surface combatants, the counting rules used in the FY 2013 budget materials are used, with an FY 2012 total of 110 ships. All combat logistics ships, support ships, and small surface combatants (mine countermeasures ships) are also considered in indirect support of the major combatants listed.

With these force structure decisions made, the team set about breaking down the Navy O&M budget, the most disaggregated budget of all the services. Air Operations, Ship Operations, Combat Operations Support, and Weapons are each in their own Activity Group, with SAGs within each. This required a matrix approach that went beyond simply dividing up all of the direct and indirect forces on a personnel basis. Each line item was matrixed against the units to which it applied. For example, "Cruise missile" SAG costs need to be applied to SSNs and destroyers but not amphibious ships.

All Air Operations line items were applied to naval aviation and aircraft carriers. All Ship Operations were applied to the surface and undersea fleets, based on number of personnel on each ship. Combat Operations Support and Weapons Support were applied generally across the entire set of force structure elements, with exceptions when clearly applicable to only specific platforms (e.g., ballistic missiles to SSBNs). Naval Special Warfare Teams costs were based on personnel reported as special operations by SOCOM in its budget materials, with the relative level of SOCOM O&M added on.

The final challenge was to deal with an issue raised in the working group that Marine aviation support costs accrue to the Navy. To this end, the team took all O&M for aviation and divided it by plane (based on personnel attributed to each plane type), including both Marine aircraft and Navy aircraft, then moved the O&M for Marine aircraft into the Marine Air Group costs seen below. This is the only case where costs from one service were moved to another.

Marine Corps

The Marine Corps is a difficult service for which to quantify costs because of its innate ties to the Navy. Therefore, it should be understood that the costs attributed here are those specifically attributed to the Marine Corps in budget documents in almost all cases. So the amphibious ships that the Marines frequently operate off of but that are owned and operated by the Navy remain attributed to the Navy. The base force structure units used here, as in the CBO study of force structure, are regiments and the regimental air groups. While the Marines also separate themselves into different units—Marine Expeditionary Forces (MEF), Marine Expeditionary Units (MEU), and Marine Air Group Task Forces (MAGTF)—the regiment level provided enough variability to make force structure decisions that would not immediately cut the service to the bone. Discussions with experts also suggested that the regiment-sized units are the relative size at which the Marines most commonly deploy.

Once the force structure layout was determined, the Marines were relatively easy to divide up, as they have relatively few dedicated budget line items. All combat units come out of the "Operating Forces" line item, and there are no indirect cost line items. Significant indirect costs are likely born by the Navy, but these could not be separated out. Costs were divided up by the unit sizes of regiments and air groups. The one attribution of Navy costs to the Marine Corps came in the air groups (as noted above), where O&M for Marine aircraft was moved out of the Navy based on the number and types of aircraft operated by the Marines.

Finally, Marine Special Operations battalions were based on the number of special operations personnel, divided by the number of battalions (three), with support costs attributed based on the same per-person methodology as above, with defense-wide SOCOM O&M added on top.

Air Force

Like the Navy, the Air Force's force structure is centered on its platforms. Force structure units are rolled up into platform types: fighters, bombers, tankers, lift, and unmanned ISR. On top of these are the additional Air Force responsibilities for strategic forces (ICBMs) and space assets. Although some of these platforms could be considered support assets, it was decided among the study team that all of these platforms provide significant capability that needed to be both displayed and variable in the 2021 force cost calculator. The primary combat forces and strategic forces are lumped together in the budget materials, funding all fighter, bomber, and strike assets, as well as the three ICBM wings with 150 ballistic missiles each. ISR assets and special operations forces are funded in the indirect combat enhancement forces. Space operations are in their own activity group, as are all mobility operations.

Using the platforms as the basis for force structure led to using per-aircraft personnel as the basis for dividing costs between aircraft types (e.g., B-2, F-22) within each funding stream (e.g., space, mobility). Therefore, while the force structure decisions are being made at the platform type level (e.g., bombers), these decisions can drill back down to the platform level (e.g., B-52). Every airframe in the Air Force was not costed separately. This analysis focused on major platforms and attributed some of the other air frames, including smaller transport aircraft, rotary aircraft, AWACS, and trainers as in indirect support of the major platform capability. The major platforms were the B-1, B-2, B-52, A-10, F-15, F-16, F-22, F-35, C-130, C-17, C-5, KC-10, KC-135, KC-46, MQ-1, MQ-9, and RQ-4. Aircraft counts came from the Air Force, and the unit of measure was Primary Mission Aircraft Inventory (PMAI): the combat-coded aircraft allocated for the performance of wartime missions. This count excludes many aircraft designated for training, testing, attrition reserve, and other noncombat roles. The study team decided that PMAI best described the amount of combat power that can be brought to bear and that other non-combat-coded aircraft could be considered as the required backup and support to keep that number of combat aircraft available.

Space systems were treated differently. The costs and number of personnel attributed to space and launch operations were determined by the line items for these activities in the budget materials, as well as the Global C3I & Early Warning SAG. These two sets of costs encompass the full range of what the study team dubbed the Global Force Enabling Architecture of land-based and space-based ISR assets, including military satellite communications, ballistic missile warning, tactical warning surveillance, satellite launch support, imaging, GPS, weather, air traffic control, and other capabilities. Given the inability to disaggregate the costs for any particular type of radar system or satellite constellation, the study team treated this system as a level of effort, meaning that the costs expended in 2012 were used as the baseline of "effort," measured in dollars, of "1." Therefore, if DoD were to spend half again as much on these enablers, this analysis would display that as 1.5 units of Global Force Enabling Architecture. Given the constellation nature of some of these types of assets, it is understood that simply cutting funding by X percent is not a tenable action. Any cuts here would have to be targeted. The CSIS team saw the ISR capabilities provided by these systems as key in all future security environments and thus at least preserved, if not increased, spending in this area.

Defense-Wide

The direct, indirect, and operational support cost division described above was critical to both understanding the costs inside of each service and applying them as correctly as possible across to each force structure unit. It was at this point that Defense-Wide operational O&M costs ($2 billion) were shared among each of the force structure units based on the total number of direct and indirect personnel in that unit. Also, the $4 billion in SO-COM costs were applied to SOF in each service. With that final step done, the entirety of the operational O&M and MilPers budgets were accounted for in force structure. Although the segmentation into direct, indirect, and operational support costs was necessary for the bottom-up work necessary to cost force structure units, it was tangential to the big picture work to come in trading between whole units. With the force cost models built for each service, the study team turned to aggregating this information into a consolidated 2012 cost for each force structure unit in each service.

With the entirety of the operational force attributed to force structure units, the next step was to take these 2012 fully costed units and apply the internal cost growth discussed earlier to their personnel and O&M costs and turn them into 2021 units. The outputs of this can be seen in Table D-1, which shows the impact of 15 percent cost growth on those force structure costs.

With the 2021 costs established, the 2021 Force Cost Calculator could now be used to look at alternative force structures in 2021 based on different strategic trade-offs.

An illustrative copy of the calculator can be seen in Table D-2. The 2021 Unit Cost column multiplied by the number of force structure units must be reduced by $43 billion in order to reach the BCA caps level of funding. Also included is an illustrative "sequester force" that showed how cuts would look if applied evenly across the board to each force structure unit. The final blank column is where users could input the number of force structure units in their vision of a 2021 strategy, and the total at the bottom would sum the total costs of that force.

With the 2021 Force Cost Calculator complete, the second calculator needed to be built in order to account for the second stage of decision-making: modernization.

Developing the 2012–2021 Modernization Calculator

With the completion of the 2021 Force Cost Calculator, the team needed to turn to the second aggregation of operational costs: those for modernization. Since 1973, the beginning of the all-volunteer force, the average percentage of the total defense budget taken up by modernization was 32.8 percent. The study team underwent many discussions of the proper treatment of modernization during a drawdown. During previous drawdowns, the modernization accounts have been treated as the bill payers for budget cuts because they are the easiest to cut quickly and to defer to later years. During the drawdown after the Carter-Reagan buildup, these investment accounts accounted for 60 percent of the total cut, despite making up only 35 percent of the budget. There was discussion of cutting the percentage of the budget allotted to the modernization accounts to better simulate the traditional mode of cutting the budget. The study team decided, in the end, that preserving

Table D-1. Inflating Costs into the 2021 Force

Force Structure Units	No. of 2012 Force Structure Units	2012 Unit Cost (constant $M)	2021 Unit Cost (constant $M)
Active Army			
Heavy BCT	17	$1,084	$1,296
Infantry BCT	20	$1,009	$1,207
Stryker BCT	8	$1,232	$1,473
Army SOF Battalions	23	$235	$280
Combat Aviation Brigades	12	$532	$638
Army Reserve Component			
Heavy BCT	7	$751	$915
Infantry BCT	20	$697	$849
Stryker BCT	1	$844	$1,029
Combat Aviation Brigades	8	$483	$601
Active Navy			
Aircraft Carriers (Excluding Aviation)	11	$1,254	$1,447
Surface Combatants	110	$91	$115
Amphibious Ships	30	$241	$306
Nuclear Attack Submarines (SSN)	54	$79	$100
Ballistic Missile Submarines (SSBN)	14	$134	$170
Missile Submarines (SSGN)	4	$134	$170
Naval Aviation	10	$1,236	$1,568
Naval Special Warfare Teams	15	$112	$137
Active Marine Corps			
Infantry Regiments	11	$1,264	$1,547
Marine Air Groups	11	$477	$585
Special Operations Battalions	3	$180	$219
Active Air Force			
Bombers	96	$69	$83
Fighters	648	$24	$29
Transport/Tankers	438	$30	$36
Aerial ISR	215	$9	$11
Special Operations Battalions	5	$916	$1,117
ICBMs	450	$6	$8
Global Force Enabling Architecture	1	$4,756	$5,825
Air Force Reserve Component			
Fighters	450	$10	$13
Transport/Tanker	516	$17	$21

Table D-2. Blank 2021 Force Cost Calculator

Force Structure Units	2021 Unit Cost	2012 Force Structure Units	2021 Sequester Force	2021 Strategic Options
Active Army				
Heavy BCT	$1,296	17	14.6	—
Infantry BCT	$1,207	20	17.2	—
Stryker BCT	$1,473	8	6.9	—
Army SOF Battalions	$280	23	19.8	—
Combat Aviation Brigades	$638	12	10.3	—
Army Reserve Component				
Heavy BCT	$915	7	6.0	—
Infantry BCT	$849	20	17.2	—
Stryker BCT	$1,029	1	0.9	—
Combat Aviation Brigades	$601	8	6.9	—
Active Navy				
Aircraft Carriers (Excluding Aviation)	$1,447	11	9.5	—
Surface Combatants	$115	110	94.7	—
Amphibious Ships	$306	30	25.8	—
Nuclear Attack Submarines (SSN)	$100	54	46.5	—
Ballistic Missile Submarines (SSBN)	$170	14	12.1	—
Missile Submarines (SSGN)	$170	4	3.4	—
Naval Aviation	$1,568	10	8.6	—
Naval Special Warfare Teams	$137	15	12.9	—
Active Marine Corps				
Infantry Regiments	$1,547	11	9.5	—
Marine Air Groups	$585	11	9.5	—
Special Operations Battalions	$219	3	2.6	—
Active Air Force				
Bombers	$83	96	82.7	—
Fighters	$29	648	557.9	—
Transport/Tankers	$36	438	377.1	—
Aerial ISR	$11	215	185.1	—
Special Operations Battalions	$1,117	5	4.3	—
Global Force Enabling Architecture		1	0.9	—
Air Force Reserve Component				
Fighters	$13	450	387.5	—
Transport/Tanker	$21	516	444.3	—
TOTAL COST		$269,886,849,264	$226,546,765,137	$0

a technologically advanced force with a commitment to investment in the future force was the right way to cut; thus, the team maintained a historically based share of the budget for modernization. Nonetheless, when discussing strategic options, this share could change in choosing different options that emphasize different priorities and aspects of the future force.

This analysis assumes that the share of the three accounts, Procurement, RDT&E, and Military Construction, inside the amount allotted to modernization is fixed through 2021. Similarly to modernization as a whole, this could be altered based on strategic options, but for the baseline force, this ratio is fixed.

Once modernization was separated into Institutional Support and Operational Force, the study team had to decide how to make modernization decisions for 2021. The modernization accounts are composed of over 2,000 individual budget lines in each year, and they change each year based on the programs in development and in production that year. After pulling out the institutional modernization (foundational S&T funding, industrial capacity, nontactical vehicles, support equipment, etc.), the next step was to separate and define the modernization that needed to be specifically targeted for decision making—the large programs that would be crucial for demonstrating trade-offs.

The move to focusing on large programs is not insignificant. In any given year, approximately 65 percent of all modernization goes to line items outside of these major programs. Of this 65 percent, half is captured by institutional support activities (including all Mil-Con). The other half is operational modernization that is of smaller systems, smaller programs, modifications to existing platforms, subsystems, munitions, and myriad other items, which get lumped together as "minor" modernization. This study assumes that minor procurement varies evenly with the total modernization budget (which in turn varies with the budget topline).

For the purposes of developing a foundation for making trade-offs, the team focused on the Major Defense Acquisition Programs (MDAPs). MDAPs are those programs designated by the Under Secretary of Defense (Acquisition, Technology, and Logistics) as programs estimated to require over the life of the program an expenditure for RDT&E of more than $365 million (in FY 2000 constant dollars) or, for procurement, of more than $2.19 billion.[8] The costs and plans for these programs are broken out by year in the Selected Acquisition Reports (SARs). Each program has the Procurement, RDT&E, and MilCon costs associated with it, on an annual basis, identified out to the end of the program. In recent experience, MDAPs have made up 35 percent of the modernization budget, and that is the amount allocated in the CSIS baseline. The study used the SARs published in December 2012 as the baseline of the programs inside of the modernization accounts on which to make decisions. In 2012, there were 82 MDAPs broken out in the SARs.

---

8. Defense Acquisition University, *ACQuipedia*, https://dap.dau.mil/acquipedia/Pages/ArticleDetails.aspx?aid=a201ded6-44cd-4cba-8bf5-e755f114c1cf.

Having limited the tradespace in modernization to the MDAPs, it quickly became clear that modernization could not be treated simply as a point in time for 2021 like force structure. Force structure cuts could be dealt with in a linear drawing-down fashion, but modernization had high variance year to year between what was actually being purchased. In addition, by relying on the MDAPs, which exist only for current large programs, the farther away from the base year (2012), the more programs dropped off the plan and thus the lower the total value of the sum of the programs in the out-years. So if the intermediate years were ignored, the MDAP portion of the 2021 budget would be well under the amount of budget available for MDAPs.

One way to mitigate this recency bias would be to add in potential future programs expected to fill that future gap. This would add the benefit of showing additional future capability trade-offs but also engage in significant speculation about what future investments might be sought. In service to this issue, the study team identified two significant future programs not in the MDAPs now that will have a major impact on funding trade-offs due to their key capabilities and high costs. These are the Ohio-class ballistic missile submarine replacement (SSBN(X)) and the new long-range strike bomber (LRSB). Open source materials were used to make year-by-year funding profiles for these two programs. Under this model, the first SSBN(X) would be procured in 2021.[9] Using budget documents and statements made by DoD, the team's profile for the LRSB would have it remain in the development stage through the study period but would enable delivery to begin in 2025. As no LRSBs are procured over the study period, this development spending is treated as a level of effort, and it can be assumed that any reduction in that level of effort would push back the initial procurement date beyond 2025. The key takeaway from this approach of using only the two exceptions is that any other MDAP that someone would want to add into the overall modernization program would have to be traded against something else already there.

In order to overcome the year-to-year variation in the amount required to execute the MDAP programs on record, the team took an aggregate of the entire study period as the tradespace for modernization. This not only mitigated the recency problem but also eliminated the question of time phasing of modernization. The modernization calculator does not address when during the study period the procurement of any given platform would occur or how many units would be procured in a given year. The calculator only identifies the number of platforms that would be procured over the total study period. Although DoD does have to concern itself with the time phasing of programs, this was outside the scope of this effort.

So to build a modernization profile, initially, the team took all 82 MDAPs, summed their modernization costs over 2012–2021 (adjusted for inflation and inflated for expected cost growth), then compared that total to the amount of major modernization funding that would be available under the model described above. As the modernization calculator developed, it became clear that the full 82 programs were relatively unwieldy and that

---

9. Congressional Budget Office, *An Analysis of the Navy's Fiscal Year 2014 Shipbuilding Plan* (October 2013), http://www.cbo.gov/sites/default/files/cbofiles/attachments/44655-Shipbuilding.pdf.

most of the major muscle movements were confined to a smaller subset of programs. Therefore the calculator focused the tradespace on the 30 largest programs in cost over the study period. This encompassed every program with over $5 billion in planned spending and accounted for over 80 percent of the MDAP spending.

The total modernization program required a cut of $195 billion over 10 years. About 70 percent of that is realized through percent-based cuts in institutional and minor operational modernization. The remaining 30 percent comes from the MDAPs. In order to meet the budget caps, $54 billion had to be cut out of those 30 programs. In order to facilitate that process, the team created the modernization cost calculator, seen in Table D-3.

Table D-3. The Modernization Cost Calculator

Program	Total Cost, 2012–2021	Unit Cost, 2012–2021	2012 MDAP Procurement Plan	2021 Sequester Force
KC-46A	$27,248,654,112	$289,879,299	94	84.7
LCS	$18,904,198,569	$609,812,857	31	27.9
P-8A	$24,927,617,948	$239,688,634	104	93.7
Virginia-class SSN	$47,483,124,659	$2,967,695,291	16	14.4
V-22	$18,416,000,756	$104,045,202	177	159.5
CVN-78	$22,142,282,921	$11,071,141,461	2	1.8
DDG-51	$24,055,094,132	$2,004,591,178	12	10.8
F-35A	$64,503,937,519	$93,619,648	689	621.0
F-35B	$28,189,048,446	$215,183,576	131	118.1
F-35C	$24,241,420,024	$202,011,834	120	108.2
BMDS	$53,212,159,541	$532,121,595	100	90.1
UH-60M	$12,668,356,373	$18,993,038	667	601.2
CH-53K	$13,130,423,419	$182,366,992	72	64.9
E-2D Advanced Hawkeye	$14,386,117,663	$239,768,628	60	54.1
LRSB	$25,206,279,896	$25,206,279,896	1	0.9
SSBN(X)	$23,480,556,450	$23,480,556,450	1	0.9
SBIRS	$6,271,038,152	$3,135,519,076	2	1.8
C-130J	$5,706,469,247	$121,414,239	47	42.4
CH-47F	$6,201,850,835	$29,532,623	210	189.3
MQ-9 Reaper	$9,627,568,437	$39,296,198	245	220.8
HC/MC-130 Recap	$9,909,114,724	$117,965,651	84	75.7
WIN-T Inrement-3	$8,859,800,324	$4,655,702	1903	1,715.2
AEHF	$5,421,533,593	$2,710,766,797	2	1.8
Patriot-MEADS CAP	$5,700,519,085	$7,939,442	718	647.2
H-1 Upgrades	$7,294,172,060	$33,459,505	218	196.5
AH-64E Remanufacture	$8,957,721,954	$20,783,578	431	388.5
LHA 6	$7,062,157,450	$7,062,157,450	1	0.9
SM-6	$6,448,593,679	$4,960,457	1300	1,171.7
MQ-4C Triton	$8,260,627,921	$236,017,941	35	31.5
Trident II	$7,266,335,468	$302,763,978	24	21.6

The calculator simply took the total modernization cost for each program and divided by the actual number of units planned to be procured in that time period to create a unit cost. These unit costs will not line up exactly with reported unit costs because of procurement funding outside the study period and the additional RDT&E funding still being charged to these programs. Nonetheless, they do account for all program spending over the 10-year period. By creating a unit cost, the calculator then allows rebalancing of the modernization programs to fit a strategy and focus cuts on lower priority areas.[10] As discussed in both the main report and Appendix C, the "Sequester Force" column serves as an illustration of what the cuts look like if they were applied evenly across every program in order to reach the $53 billion in cuts necessary to get down to the topline amount available under the BCA caps.

Conclusion

The combination of these two calculators allows an observer to both trade within and between modernization and force structure in determining the right force allocation for the 2021 affordable military. The study team used the calculators to create four different outcomes focused on different strategic priorities. By switching between the two calculators, this study looks at different force mixes as well as the interplay between modernization and force structure and different ways to apply DoD's dollars to strategic ends.

Although this report represents the final step in a long process to build both this methodology and the tools used to inform strategic trade-offs, it is not the end point. This appendix will serve as a living document as the work in creating the Affordable Military continues to grow. CSIS is already looking to the next steps to push this methodology forward. The first step will be in continuing to vet and discuss the methodology and tools with senior leaders as a new way to look at the execution of a defense drawdown. In addition, CSIS will be engaging with members of the policy community as well as DoD and industry to determine valuable next steps to expanding these analytic tools. Notably, CSIS will look for ways to bring this methodology and these tools to a broader community to enable others to take their own look at how the drawdown in defense should be executed or to use different assumptions and priorities. CSIS will be looking to develop this into a web-based application to encourage broader participation.

Managing the defense drawdown today is as important a challenge to U.S. national security as any, and involving more people in that debate will be key to making informed decisions to maintain U.S. military superiority.

---

10. An important caveat is that industrial base and contract-based issues were not heavily considered. Changing procurement quantities, ramp rates, and time phasing can have significant impacts in unit cost. In addition, terminating or breaking contracts can add additional costs through penalties. These issues were not incorporated into the calculator. The only area where this was noted was in preventing the purchase of old platforms no longer in production (e.g., buying B-2s, even though the production line has long been shut down).

Appendix E. Adapting to 2020+ Strategic Realities[1]

Angela Weaver

The Department of Defense is an adaptive organization that will not mindlessly sustain today's force into 2020 and beyond (2020+) as it draws down its budget to meet the caps imposed by the Budget Control Act of 2011 (BCA). Even if it adheres to the priorities first set in the 2012 Defense Strategic Guidance (DSG) and reinforced in the 2014 Quadrennial Defense Review (QDR), the Department will adapt the force to address evolving security threats and the changing nature of war. The Department will also preserve critical U.S. competencies, such as its high-tech advantage, and sustain the high standards of readiness that make the U.S. military the world's finest. In recognition of DoD's inherent adaptability, the 2021 Baseline Force is not just a smaller version of today's force but one that has been flexible enough to adapt to the evolving strategic realities in 2021 and beyond.

This appendix will outline the security environment in which the United States will be operating, identify the threats the United States is likely to face in the coming decade, and explore the implications of these factors for U.S. defense priorities and capabilities. It will also identify American military competencies that DoD will seek to sustain. This examination will provide a context in which U.S. defense and policy planners will address future security demands (also referred to as the "demand function"[2]), resulting in a demand-driven list of "must-have capabilities" needed by the 2021 Affordable Military.

---

1. This appendix was shaped by the Defense Drawdown Working Group paper entitled "The 2020+ Security Environment: Describing the Demand Function for the 2021 Affordable Force," written by Kelley Sayler, former research associate at CSIS.

2. The demand function is composed of multiple factors: the potential threats to American interests, the future security environment in which military missions are likely to be executed, and the partnership capacity that could be called on for assistance. See Kelley Sayler, "The 2020+ Security Environment: Describing the Demand Function for the 2021 Affordable Force," CSIS, December 10, 2012, http://csis.org/files/publication/121210_painting_picture.pdf.

Near-Peer Competitors: China and Russia

While the United States will remain a premier global power, the increasingly bold actions of Russia and the rising strength and influence of China (anticipated by the U.S. shift to the Asia-Pacific) will become a driving force in how the United States perceives, and adjusts to, the future security environment.

Russia

As the 2014 QDR states, "the United States is willing to undertake security cooperation with Russia, both in the bilateral context and in seeking solutions to regional challenges" and "will engage Russia to increase transparency and reduce the risk of military miscalculation."[3] As has been demonstrated by Russian actions in the Syrian and Ukrainian crises, Russia is determined to remain a state with global power and influence, even at the cost of violating the sovereignty of neighboring states. Low-level conventional provocations by Russia are likely to continue as President Putin continues to test the mettle of the United States and its NATO allies.

The importance of nuclear weapons in the relationship between Russia and the United States is still critical. Russia's reliance on its nuclear arsenal stems from a severe lack of conventional capability and has dominated both its defense planning and budget. In the years ahead, Russia will continue to modernize its nuclear arsenal in an effort to meet its defense and deterrence requirements and operate under a posture of coercive nuclear diplomacy in order to maintain its spheres of influence and its position on the world stage. The March 2014 intercontinental ballistic missile test, though in accordance with START Treaty notification policies, showed continued commitment to Russia's "multi-dimensional defense modernization."[4] Recent Russian actions with regard to Crimea and Ukraine further show the actions Russia is willing to take when backed by a significant nuclear arsenal.

IMPLICATIONS FOR U.S. DEFENSE

Given these actions, maintaining parity with Russia in terms of nuclear forces is essential to sustaining strategic stability. The United States will not only need to maintain the nuclear arsenal at current levels but must pursue modernization programs that will allow the arsenal to remain "safe, secure, and effective"[5] into 2030 and beyond. Ballistic missile defense (BMD) will continue to be a sticking point with Russia, as the United States continues to invest in early warning systems and defensive interceptors, making the strength of the U.S. nuclear deterrent all the more important. Russia must be convinced through this

---

3. Department of Defense (DoD), *Quadrennial Defense Review 2014* (Washington, D.C.: DoD, 2014), 6, http://www.defense.gov/pubs/2014_Quadrennial_Defense_Review.pdf.
4. Ibid.
5. DoD, *Nuclear Posture Review* Report (Washington, D.C.: DoD, April 2010), 37, http://www.defense.gov/npr/docs/2010%20nuclear%20posture%20review%20report.pdf.

deterrent relationship to "behave as a 'responsible stakeholder' in regional affairs, and additionally provide a source of strategic stability in bilateral relations."[6]

China and the Asia-Pacific

The Asia-Pacific region is an increasing focus of U.S. foreign policy as defense spending in the region continues to rise and technological, military, and security capabilities improve. Creating and maintaining stability in a region that is experiencing growing military and technological capability is essential to preventing crisis escalation. Long-standing sovereignty and territorial disputes, such as that over the Senkaku Islands, have the potential to become destabilizing conflicts as tensions between states like Japan and China continue to grow.

China, in particular, has become increasingly assertive over disputes such as these and has demonstrated the willingness to challenge foreign governments with escalatory actions, such as the establishment of the Air Defense Identification Zone (ADIZ) over the East China Sea in November 2013. If China continues to provoke regional tensions and disputes, there is increased possibility of rapid crisis escalation and, very likely, armed conflict.

China has accelerated the modernization of its military, most notably investing in greater A2/AD capabilities and developing new missile launch sites and underground storage facilities for its nuclear weapons arsenal. China is believed to already possess a nuclear-capable missile arsenal including silo-based, liquid-fueled ICBMs and solid-fueled road-mobile ICBMs (among others), submarine-launched ballistic missiles, and short-range ballistic missiles.[7] China continues to pursue more advanced cyber capabilities as well, which can pose a threat to U.S. cyber and space assets.

IMPLICATIONS FOR U.S. DEFENSE

Greater stability in the region could be achieved through more transparency concerning Chinese capabilities and intentions.[8] However, in the absence of this, the United States must rely on an ability to project power and maintain forward presence for the sake of U.S. allies in the region. Sustaining a nuclear arsenal that both assures regional allies under the nuclear umbrella and maintains deterrence with China is necessary for stability and crisis management. Improved space and cyber protections and capabilities will help hedge in the face of improving Chinese capabilities in these domains. Although the likelihood of armed conflict with China is low (barring any rapidly escalating crises over territory), competition and the potential for conflict in the areas of space and cyber will continue to grow in the years to come.

---

6. Sayler, "The 2020+ Security Environment," 11.
7. Nuclear Threat Initiative, "China Overview," http://www.nti.org/country-profiles/china/nuclear/.
8. DoD, *Quadrennial Defense Review 2014*, 4.

North Korea

The North Korean regime will continue to be a destabilizing force in the Northeast Asian region as long as its pursuit of nuclear weapons continues; nuclear weapons represent the core of North Korea's national security strategy and constitute the internal image of the regime as a legitimate global power, making it unlikely that the program will be eliminated willingly. Additionally, the regime's robust ballistic missile arsenal and large conventional capabilities create a significant security issue for the region, especially South Korea, as well as a challenge to U.S. extended deterrence. North Korea is believed to have between 175 and 200 Nodong missiles (1,300 km; medium to intermediate range), an unknown number of Scud-C ballistic missiles (500 km; short-range), and an unknown number of anti-ship cruise missiles.[9] A force structure of this size could certainly be used in an offensive strike against South Korea and serves as a valuable deterrent to the regime.

Following the regime's third nuclear test in 2013, the United States flew two nuclear-capable stealth bombers (B-2 Spirits) over the Korean peninsula to "show America's ability to conduct long-range, precision strikes 'quickly and at will.'"[10] This was an important step in exercising U.S. extended deterrence on the Korean peninsula; however, as the regime continues to build its ballistic missile and nuclear weapon force, South Korea and Japan will continue to look to U.S. extended deterrence to counter the growing threat in North Korea. As North Korea's greatest ally, China will play an important role in events on the Korean peninsula in the years to come as well. Following the third nuclear test, Chinese patience with the regime seems to be running thin. Regardless, the U.S. relationship with China will affect Chinese decisions with regard to North Korea.

IMPLICATIONS FOR U.S. DEFENSE

The 2014 QDR identified the North Korean nuclear program as a "growing, direct threat to the United States."[11] A viable U.S. nuclear deterrent is necessary in attempting to tamp the rhetoric and actions of the regime. Not only does the nuclear program threaten U.S. security and interests directly, but it threatens the stability and security of a region where U.S. allies reside. The United States must be willing to press the Chinese to take a tougher stance when it comes to their unpredictable neighbor and ally. U.S. extended deterrence is a key part of the U.S. relationship with allies in Northeast Asia and Europe. Effective responses to North Korean provocations in the coming years will be vital to maintaining allied faith in U.S. extended deterrence. The U.S. ability to respond to this growing threat in the coming years will require an effective nuclear deterrent and a conventional force capable of responding quickly and decisively (e.g., Marine assault operations, Navy littoral combat forces, U.S. Special Forces) in the event the United States must provide military assistance to the South.[12]

---

9. Nuclear Threat Initiative, "North Korea Overview," http://www.nti.org/country-profiles/north-korea/.

10. David Chance and Phil Stewart, "North Korea Readies Missiles after U.S. Stealth Bombers Fly over South," Reuters, March 29, 2013, http://uk.reuters.com/article/2013/03/29/uk-korea-north-idUK-BRE92R13Q20130329.

11. DoD, *Quadrennial Defense Review 2014*, 4.

12. Sayler, "The 2020+ Security Environment," 7.

South and Central Asia

Pakistan-U.S. relations will become increasingly important as the United States shapes its foreign policy in the coming decade. The U.S. drawdown in Afghanistan places extra stress on the relationship, as the United States will increasingly depend on Pakistani support in the region to maintain stability. Although U.S. and Pakistani interests do not always align, strategic stability in the region will require cooperation between the two. However, U.S. concerns over growing regional terrorism as well as an unstable relationship between Pakistan and India, made more complicated by nuclear weapons, will continue to plague the relationship.

The unpredictability of the region threatens the security of Pakistan's stockpile and creates a more complicated proliferation challenge for the United States; in the event of a crisis or state collapse, "Pakistan's policy of storing its weapons in component form, which guards against accidental launch," makes the theft of nuclear material, by a terrorist organization or otherwise, much more likely.[13] The United States' concern over terrorist activities in the region is directly tied to the amount of fissile material being produced in Pakistan, and if Pakistan continues to produce at today's levels, the threat of theft or diversion of nuclear material will grow.[14] As David Sanger and Eric Schmitt point out, Pakistan rejects any effort to undermine its strategic deterrence, as deterring India remains a national security priority for the Pakistani leadership.[15] Maintaining strategic stability in the region is essential if any U.S. effort to slow down fissile material production in Pakistan is to succeed.

China also plays a significant role in South Asian security dynamics, especially as a player in what is known as the "strategic triangle."[16] The nuclear relationships that exist between China, India, and Pakistan all consist of different dynamics. Toby Dalton puts it this way: "As the dominant competitor, China sits at the apex of the triangle. . . . The Sino-Indian leg is competitive; the Sino-Pakistani leg is cooperative. Developments on one leg influence what happens in others."[17] China has had a history of cooperation with Pakistan. Continued U.S. involvement with Pakistan into the future may exacerbate tension with China that could have consequences with regard to the South Asian strategic triangle, especially if Indo-Pak hostility continues.

IMPLICATIONS FOR U.S. DEFENSE

Although the U.S. nuclear arsenal is an effective deterrent against aggression, it does not solve the underlying strategic competition between Pakistan and India, further complicated by China. The U.S. relationships with China and Pakistan will play a large role in any crisis

---

13. Ibid., 10.

14. Pakistan also has a history of supplying nuclear technology to states such as North Korea, which makes the production of large amounts of fissile material and technology of even greater concern.

15. David E. Sanger and Eric Schmitt, "Pakistani Nuclear Arms Pose Challenge to U.S. Policy," *New York Times*, January 31, 2011, http://www.nytimes.com/2011/02/01/world/asia/01policy.html?pagewanted=all&_r=0.

16. Toby Dalton, "Strategic Triangle," *Force*, August 2013, http://www.forceindia.net/StrategicTriangle.aspx.

17. Ibid.

that may occur in this region and, if regime collapse in Pakistan were to occur, the United States would most certainly feel a need to rapidly respond. This would likely include military personnel on the ground. U.S. ability to swiftly project power and remain present for sustained periods of time is essential to the success of this type of response.

Iran and the Broader Middle East

The Middle East has been a focal point of U.S. foreign policy for over a decade and, even with the shift to Asia, the region will continue to demand attention from policymakers. Recent events, such as the civil war in Syria, a potentially widening religious divide between Sunni and Shi'a, the cyclically tense Arab-Israeli conflict, and the proliferation (and use in Syria) of weapons of mass destruction (WMD), will continue to foster instability, making this region an enduring security issue for U.S. interests and allies.[18]

Iran is a destabilizing influence in the Middle East, due to its continued pursuit of nuclear weapons, hostility toward Israel, and repeated opposition to U.S. actions in the Middle East. The U.S. intervention in Iraq and Afghanistan and Iran's geographic location on the Strait of Hormuz have contributed to a higher threat perception by the Iranians and their apparent desire to obtain nuclear weapons as a deterrent against U.S. intervention or invasion.[19] The Iranian nuclear program not only presents a proliferation prevention challenge but makes U.S. allies in the region, particularly Israel, very nervous. Israeli Prime Minister Benjamin Netanyahu has referred to the Iranian nuclear program as the "Pandora's box"[20] of proliferation in the Middle East and has not ruled out preemptive strikes on Iranian nuclear facilities. A preemptive strike, by Israel or otherwise, would be an extremely destabilizing event.

Although productive steps have been taken to address this proliferation challenge, the most significant being the interim deal reached in November 2013, a long-term agreement has yet to be reached. The United States has consistently stated that all options are on the table with regard to the program, leaving a preemptive strike or other form of military intervention as a viable option. Preventing a nuclear Iran will be an important U.S. priority, as failure to do so could result in an emboldened Iran willing to become further involved in more destabilizing activities in the region (greater involvement in state-sponsored terrorism, crisis escalation, etc.) and, possibly, a proliferation cascade in the Middle East.[21]

The friction points in the broader Middle East will continue to present security challenges to the United States as instability and tensions in the region grow. The ongoing Syrian conflict presents several challenges to stability, the expansion of global jihad being one of the most significant. The outcome of this conflict will greatly affect the security

---

18. Nora Bensahel and Daniel L. Byman, eds., *The Future Security Environment in the Middle East: Conflict, Stability, and Political Change* (Santa Monica, CA: RAND, 2004), http://www.rand.org/content/dam/rand/pubs/monograph_reports/2005/MR1640.pdf.
19. Sayler, "The 2020+ Security Environment," 7.
20. CBS/AP, "Netanyahu: Nuclear Iran Would Open a 'Pandora's Box' of Proliferation," CBS News, March 4, 2014, http://www.cbsnews.com/news/netanyahu-nuclear-iran-would-open-a-pandoras-box-of-proliferation/.
21. Sayler, "The 2020+ Security Environment," 8.

environment of the region moving forward, and the United States has an interest in seeing stability return. The stability of Iraq and Afghanistan are also of great concern to the United States, especially as U.S. forces depart. Political instability in Egypt and tensions between Palestinians and Israelis will remain long-term concerns of the United States.

IMPLICATIONS FOR U.S. DEFENSE

U.S. and allied interests in this region (over oil, resources, proliferation prevention, and terrorism) are critical to national security, and given the likelihood of a crisis or breakdown in stability, the United States will need to have a military capable of rapid deployment of ground troops, special operations forces (SOF), and possible prolonged military presence. The ability to assure allies and partners in the region will directly correlate to the U.S. ability to respond swiftly to crises and deter aggression. Conventional strength, especially that capable of responding to the size and depth of Iran's conventional forces, will be essential to succeed in this goal.[22] Because of the strategic importance of the Strait of Hormuz, the Navy will need to be prepared to respond as effectively to threats in this region as U.S. ground forces and special operations forces. Intelligence, Surveillance, and Reconnaissance (ISR) must be modern and capable enough to provide responsiveness to all threats in the region, including counterterrorism operations.

Terrorism and Islamic Extremists

Al Qaeda and other Islamic extremist groups, some state-sponsored, are expanding within the Middle East, seeking recruits and funding.[23] The 2014 QDR identifies terrorism as a persistent and evolving threat and suggests that "our ability to project forces to combat terrorism . . . reduces the likelihood that these threats could find their way to U.S. shores."[24] The potential for terrorist attacks and other rapidly developing threats to escalate into crises that threaten U.S. interests, citizens, and allies "is a significant challenge for the United States."[25] The ongoing conflict in Syria is creating a breeding ground for terrorist activities. In testimony presented to the House Armed Services Committee in November 2013, Brian Jenkins of RAND stated that terrorism "has become a dominant feature of Syria's civil war, which will deepen sectarian tensions throughout the region."[26]

IMPLICATIONS FOR U.S. DEFENSE

While the United States works to build partnership capacities in states where terrorism is bred and funded, the U.S. military must retain the ability to independently detect terrorist

---

22. Ibid.
23. Bensahel and Byman, *The Future Security Environment in the Middle East*, 2–3.
24. DoD, *Quadrennial Defense Review*, vi.
25. Ibid., 8.
26. Brian Michael Jenkins, "The Role of Terrorism and Terror in Syria's Civil War," testimony presented before the House Foreign Affairs Committee, Subcommittee on Terrorism, Nonproliferation, and Trade, November 20, 2013, 2, http://docs.house.gov/meetings/FA/FA18/20131120/101513/HHRG-113-FA18-Wstate-JenkinsB-20131120.pdf.

threats and retain "robust capability for direct action" against these threats.[27] To be successful in this, the United States will need to place priority on investing in more SOF, more SOF-like general purpose forces, force projection, ISR, and precision strike. Counterterror operations must be able to detect, disrupt, and defeat al Qaeda and other Islamic extremist groups and counter various other emerging transnational threats.

Changes in the Nature of Warfare

Warfare in the 21st century and in the decades moving forward will be affected by the rise of individual states, evolving technologies, and new environments. Though the United States is likely to remain the preeminent military power,[28] the rising influence (and confidence) of states like China and Russia will continue to challenge the United States in areas where the nature of warfare is rapidly changing.

Cyber and space are the two main areas in which countries such as China and Russia are pursuing technology and capabilities that can damage U.S. infrastructure, threaten U.S. security, and exacerbate international tensions or crises. Chemical and biological weapons proliferation (and use) has also been identified as a security concern for the future. Events of the type that took place in Syria as well as the threat of chemical or biological terrorist attacks against the United States and its allies are of the greatest concern.

Cyber

Cyber warfare poses an increasing threat and challenge to U.S. national security. The difficulty of attribution alone makes it an attractive domain for attack, but it also presents the opportunity to quickly disable and damage essential communication networks, infrastructure, and the capability to perform national security functions, all of which are of core importance to the United States. Cyber attacks are relatively inexpensive and, because of the difficulty in attributing them, offer a less risky form of propaganda, coercion, theft, or attack for potential U.S. adversaries. Cyber also creates a challenge in identifying clearly the differences between state, state-sponsored, and nonstate adversaries.[29]

IMPLICATIONS FOR U.S. DEFENSE

In February 2014, U.S. Army General Keith Alexander, head of U.S. Cyber Command, confirmed that "threats to our nation in cyberspace are growing" and observed that the United States is "not ready for them."[30] In the fall of 2013, Cyber Command was still in the process

---

27. DoD, *Quadrennial Defense Review*, vii.

28. Development, Concepts and Doctrine Centre (DCDC), *Global Strategic Trends—Out to 2040*, 4th ed. (London: UK Ministry of Defence, February 2010), 10, https://www.gov.uk/government/uploads/system/uploads/attachment_data/file/33717/GST4_v9_Feb10.pdf.

29. Ibid., 15.

30. Bill Gertz, "Commander: U.S. Military Not Ready for Cyber Warfare," *Washington Free Beacon*, February 27, 2014, http://freebeacon.com/national-security/commander-u-s-military-not-ready-for-cyber-warfare/.

of determining a "better conceptual idea of what is offense and what is defense" in the area of cyber.[31] The offensive cyber capabilities of states around the world, including adversaries, are improving and evolving quickly. In order to defend against these, the United States will not only need to strengthen the policies surrounding cyber but will need to simultaneously develop robust cyber defenses that provide a viable deterrent against state-sponsored and private attacks.

Space

The United States relies on space-based assets, for both commercial and military purposes (communications, ISR, navigation, etc.), more than other global powers, especially China. Much like the threats the United States faces with cyber, threats to U.S. space assets are evolving and, owing to the difficulty of attribution, are increasingly attractive to adversaries.

The Chinese not only approach space with very different eyes, as John Grady notes, but have "made enormous investments in jamming" and are better prepared to engage with adversaries in the space domain, especially offensively.[32] U.S. command and control resides almost entirely in commercial and military satellites that are largely unprotected, creating a large vulnerability problem for U.S. military capabilities in domains outside of space and cyber. The U.S. satellite system is simply "too concentrated in capability and too limited in number" to withstand any substantial attack.[33] Although nuclear weapons and any other WMD are banned from use in space per the Outer Space Treaty, there is no treaty that prohibits the use of conventional weapons in space or on space assets,[34] further complicating the issue. Russia and China are already developing abilities to field antisatellite systems, and many other states are, and will continue, pursuing technology that disrupts or destroys space assets and systems.

IMPLICATIONS FOR U.S. DEFENSE

As with cyber, the United States will need to invest in strengthening the survivability of satellites and other space assets and closely examine the strategies and policies designed to deter debilitating attacks in space that would have ramifications for capabilities in other domains. Persistent competition between technologically advanced states will certainly endure, and space and cyber will likely prove to be the domains in which limits, and deterrence, are tested. The United States must make efforts to strengthen international partnerships in the space and cyber domain. Doing so will aid in maximizing scarce

---

31. Cheryl Pellerin, "DOD Readies Elements Crucial to Cyber Operations," American Forces Press Service, June 27, 2013, http://www.defense.gov/news/newsarticle.aspx?id=120381.

32. John Grady, "U.S. Dependence on Space Assets Could Be a Liability in a Conflict with China," *USNI News*, January 29, 2014, http://news.usni.org/2014/01/29/u-s-dependence-space-assets-liability-conflict-china.

33. Ibid.

34. "Treaty on Principles Governing the Activities of States in the Exploration and Use of Outer Space, including the Moon and Other Celestial Bodies," United Nations General Assembly, Ratified 1967, http://www.oosa.unvienna.org/oosa/en/SpaceLaw/gares/html/gares_21_2222.html.

resources, mitigating collective risks, and combining each partner's core strengths to produce increased awareness and greater resilience.[35]

Chemical and Biological Weapons

There is increasing evidence to suggest that the proliferation of chemical and biological weapons (CB) is a quickly emerging threat for the future security environment; in 2009 NATO acknowledged the spread of WMD and the possibility that terrorists were actively seeking them as "principal threats to the alliance" over the next 10 to 15 years.[36] The 2014 QDR acknowledged the acquisition of WMD as a continued demonstrated interest among terrorist networks and restated the commitment of DoD in reducing the threat posed by these weapons.[37]

The ability to obtain the agents and technology required for CB production has become much less difficult, increasing the possibility for state or nonstate actors to produce them. The agents used in chemical weapons are not as regulated as nuclear material, as they are often used legitimately in other areas of research and industry, an industry that has globalized in recent years.[38] Biological weapons materials are also relatively easy to obtain and difficult to regulate as they, too, are often used in civilian biotechnology programs. The Biological and Toxin Weapons Convention (BTWC), designed to prevent the production, development, acquisition, and stockpiling of biological weapons, is highly ineffective as it "lacks verification provisions to ensure its members are not secretly maintaining biological weapons programs."[39]

Improvements in CB technology and the diffusion of technical knowledge, combined with the ease of production and stockpiling, make CB weapons an attractive, and less expensive, option for state and nonstate actors. The 2014 QDR expressed concern over "new ways of developing WMD—such as biotechnology breakthroughs," which present a proliferation risk and "fast-moving threats that are very difficult to detect and even more difficult to counter."[40] Because of these difficulties, CB use is extremely attractive to terrorist organizations willing to inflict mass panic, widespread casualties, and psychological terror. Terrorist organizations have in the past used CB attacks, such as in the 1995 Tokyo subway attack using sarin, and are known to have a continued interest in obtaining these types of WMD.

---

35. Madelyn R. Creedon, "Space and Cyber: Shared Challenges, Shared Opportunities" (edited remarks to the USSTRATCOM Cyber and Space Symposium, November 15, 2011), 6, http://www.au.af.mil/au/ssq/2012/spring/creedon.pdf.

36. "NATO's Comprehensive, Strategic-Level Policy for Preventing the Proliferation of Weapons of Mass Destruction (WMD) and Defending against Chemical, Biological, Radiological, and Nuclear (CBRN) Threats," North Atlantic Treaty Organization, September 1, 2009, http://www.nato.int/cps/en/natolive/official_texts_57218.htm.

37. DoD, *Quadrennial Defense Review 2014*, 8, 16.

38. Nuclear Threat Initiative, "Chemical Weapons," http://nti.org/threats/chemical/.

39. Nuclear Threat Initiative, "Biological Weapons," http://nti.org/threats/biological/.

40. DoD, *Quadrennial Defense Review 2014*, 8.

IMPLICATIONS FOR U.S. DEFENSE

State actors can be deterred from widespread CB use, though, as was exemplified in Syria over the summer and fall of 2013, there are exceptions. U.S. deterrence strategy and policy-makers should look at the events that transpired in Syria and create policies that attempt to deter future use on such a scale. Nonstate actors, especially those terrorist organizations interested in harming and killing U.S. citizens, are nearly impossible to deter through any traditional sense of the word. Given this, the United States will likely need to invest in greater intelligence and verification capabilities, which would allow for greater detection of CB proliferation, "passive" defense capabilities (e.g., detectors, protective garments) as well as S&T capabilities (e.g., predictive modeling),"[41] and significantly improved emergency medical responses.[42]

Sustaining Key U.S. Military Competencies

Though sustaining the priorities of today will not serve the strategy of tomorrow, the Defense Department will need to sustain some key U.S. competencies that support defense strategy in any environment. These key competencies include full-spectrum ISR, military readiness, global power projection, and military-technical superiority. Following the implementation of sequestration, the readiness of the joint force suffered and lost momentum in modernization. The 2014 QDR identified global power projection of the Air Force, operability of the Army, and modernization of the Navy as key end strength and force structure priorities, as well as modernized ISR, cyber, and space as key capabilities to maintain in support of U.S. strategy moving forward.[43]

Rapidly improving technology and the spread of information have quickly "closed the gap that existed in the past between those who created intelligence and those who operated with that intelligence."[44]As this trend continues, the link between effective intelligence and the ability to successfully project power will become stronger and therefore an increasingly important element of proficiency for the U.S. military to maintain. This will be especially important when it comes to counterterrorism operations that are persistent, networked, and effective on a global scale.

In the same way that information technology is affecting power projection and global counterterrorism, other sophisticated technologies, such as counter-stealth, are affecting the range of challenges the United States may face, altering the type and scale of responses required. Maintaining an edge in regards to technology is a fundamental strength in a world that is increasingly more globalized, commercialized, adaptable, and innovative. The United States' ability to keep pace with high-tech innovation is closely tied to its ability

---

41. Sayler, "The 2020+ Security Environment," 17.

42. Many states' emergency preparedness for CB events is "uneven" and "meager." See Nuclear Threat Initiative, "Biological Weapons," http://nti.org/threats/biological/.

43. DoD, *Quadrennial Defense Review 2014*, ix–x.

44. Lt. Gen Dave Deptula and Col. Mike Francisco, "Air Force ISR Operations," *Air and Space Power Journal* 24, no. 4 (Winter 2010): 13, file:///C:/Users/AWeaver/Downloads/ADA533656.pdf.

Figure E-1. Must-Have Capabilities Needed in 2020–2030

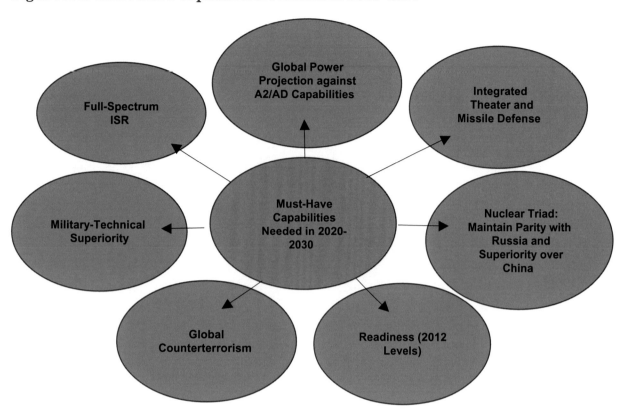

to remain globally engaged in terms of military readiness. Vice Chief of Staff of the Army General John F. Campbell fears that if sequestration continues, manning, readiness, and modernization efforts would be severely degraded and "would not allow us to execute the defense strategic guidance."[45] As Ashton Carter warned in 2001, a smaller and less capable military cannot fulfill the defense strategy of a global major power.[46]

IMPLICATIONS FOR U.S. DEFENSE

As the operating environment becomes increasingly technologically advanced, the United States will need to pursue capabilities that allow it to retain military-technical superiority. Modernization programs within each branch of the military, including updated command and control, are essential to the ability of the U.S. military to remain adaptive and high-tech. Full-spectrum ISR is among the most important, as it has the ability to support U.S. counterterrorism activities, enable greater global situational awareness, and build a stronger backbone for the modernized capabilities of the U.S. military. As Samuel Brannen noted in a recent report with Ethan Griffin and Rhys McCormick, unmanned systems and the spread of unmanned technology around the globe and into commercial applications

---

45. Terri Moon Cronk, "Military Officials Testify on Sequestration, Readiness," American Forces Press Service, April 1, 2014, http://www.af.mil/News/ArticleDisplay/tabid/223/Article/475153/military-officials-testify-on-sequestration-readiness.aspx.

46. See Ashton B. Carter, "Keeping America's Military Edge," *Foreign Affairs* (January/February 2001), http://www.foreignaffairs.com/articles/56659/ashton-b-carter/keeping-americas-military-edge.

will likely create a "multipolar, regionally complex, rapidly proliferated environment." This technology has "significant potential to continue to increase U.S. military effectiveness across a range of priority missions."[47] Global power projection and readiness will serve not only U.S. strategy in full but will allow the United States to address a broad array of threats while maintaining confidence in U.S. commitments to allies.

Must-Have U.S. Capabilities Needed in 2020–2030

The list of must-have capabilities in Figure E-1 should be viewed as a "living document" that changes as 2020+ strategic realities evolve. Changes in the international security environment, changes in the evolution of warfare, and the continuing role of nuclear weapons will continue to inform this list. The must-have capabilities list and the 2020+ strategic realities assessment that underpinned it informed the study team as it adjusted the 2021 Sequester Force to create the 2021 Baseline Force. Describing strategic realities of 2020+ was necessary in framing the study team's assessment of the strategic options, leading to the choice of Option 3: Great Power Conflict.

---

47. Samuel J. Brannen, Ethan Griffin, and Rhys McCormick, *Sustaining the U.S. Lead in Unmanned Systems* (Washington, D.C.: CSIS, February 2014), 1–2, http://csis.org/files/publication/140227_Brannen_UnmannedSystems _Web.pdf.

About the Authors

Clark Murdock is senior advisor for the Defense and National Security Group at CSIS and director of the Project on Nuclear Issues (PONI). Joining CSIS in January 2001, Murdock has completed studies on a wide range of defense and national security issues, including strategic planning, defense policy and governance, and U.S. nuclear weapons strategy and policy. He directed the four-phase study on Defense Department reform, Beyond Goldwater-Nichols: USG and Defense Reform for a New Strategic Era, which released reports in 2004, 2005, 2006, and 2008. Murdock is currently leading an ongoing "track two" dialogue on nuclear policy issues—the Trilateral Nuclear Dialogues involving the United States, United Kingdom, and France. He has also recently completed studies on methodological approaches to building force-planning constructs and on nuclear posture implications of U.S. extended deterrence and assurance. He is the principal author of *Planning for a Deep Defense Drawdown–Part 1* (CSIS, 2012; this report was the predecessor to the Affordable Military project) and *The Department of Defense and the Nuclear Mission in the 21st Century* (CSIS, 2008), and he coauthored *Nuclear Weapons in 21st Century U.S. National Security* (AAAS, 2008).

Before joining CSIS, Murdock taught courses on military strategy, the national security process, and military innovation at the National War College. Prior to that, from 1995 to 2000, he served in the Office of the Air Force Chief of Staff, where, as deputy special assistant to the chief for long-range planning, he helped develop a strategic vision for the 2020 Air Force. Then, as deputy director for strategic planning, he institutionalized the Air Force's strategic planning process and spearheaded the development of new planning products. Before joining the Air Force Chief of Staff's Office, he was special assistant to the under secretary of the Air Force, providing analytic support to the secretary and under secretary on broad issues of concern, including the future of air power and Air Force missions. Before joining the Air Force, Murdock served in the Department of Defense, where he headed the Policy Planning Staff in the Office of the Under Secretary of Defense for Policy and held responsibility for mid- to long-range analysis and planning on strategy and defense policy issues. Prior to joining the Department of Defense, he served for several years on the House Armed Services Committee as a professional staff member and as a senior policy adviser to then Chairman Les Aspin. Murdock's experience in defense planning and policy also includes service on the National Security Council as senior director for Africa affairs and in multiple roles in the Central Intelligence Agency. Before turning to government service, Murdock taught for 10 years at the State University of New York at Buffalo. He is an honors graduate of Swarthmore College and holds a PhD in political science from the University of Wisconsin at Madison.

Ryan Crotty is a fellow and deputy director for defense budget analysis with the International Security Program at CSIS. His work focuses on the management and application of defense resources, the strategic implications of resourcing decisions, and the effects of these decisions on the defense industrial base. He has worked on several CSIS projects focused on long-term defense spending trends, the defense budget drawdown and identifying challenges and opportunities facing the Department of Defense in a time of budget tightening. He also studies the interaction between the defense budget and the health of the defense industry through analysis of contracting and financial tools. He did his graduate study in international affairs at the Pennsylvania State University, where he previously worked as a research assistant to Ambassador Dennis Jett. While at Penn State, he was a 2010 recipient of the Office of the Director of National Intelligence's Strategic and Global Security Scholars Program scholarship. Previously, he worked in state government consulting in Boston, MA. He also holds a BA (with honors) in government and international studies from Colby College.

Angela Weaver is program coordinator and research assistant for the Defense and National Security Group at CSIS. Her work focuses on a wide range of defense and national security issues, including strategic planning, defense policy and governance, and U.S. nuclear weapons strategy and policy. She has written extensively on nuclear issues and strategy for the Project on Nuclear Issues blog and PONI's *Nuclear Notes*. She has also written on defense spending trends and the defense budget drawdown. She received a bachelor's degree in history from Wake Forest University, where she focused on international affairs, defense and national security policy, and interstate conflict.